Your
Rhodesian Ridgeback
Puppy

By Denise Flaim ❀ REVODANA PUBLISHING

For Fred, whelpmaster extraordinaire

REVODANA PUBLISHING
81 Lafayette Avenue, Sea Cliff, N.Y. 11579

ISBN: 978-0-9911168-3-6

Cover photo: Gijs Vos

www.revodanapublishing.com

TABLE OF CONTENTS

Are You or Aren't You?

There really are only two kinds of people in this world: Those who love Ridgebacks – and everybody else.

If you're reading this book, you are probably – luckily, happily – one of the former.

When you fall in love with a breed of dog, it's impossible to sum up in words exactly what the attraction is, any more than you can pinpoint what it was that made you fall in love with your wife, or exactly what it is about your best friend that makes her earn that adjective. It's a combination of physical presence, personality, character and some other indefinable quality, some spark.

I don't remember when the Rhodesian Ridgeback first entered my consciousness as a breed, but I do remember the day I first met one.

It was high summer in a parking lot in Montauk, on the eastern tip of Long Island. He was sitting in the shade of his owner's hot-dog truck. I think his name was Monty. He was the oversized, black-masked, red-wheaten Ridgeback cliché every novice owner wants. But he was, nonetheless, majestic. And he granted my husband and me an audience in that sand-strewn oceanside lot with equal amounts dignity and dispassion.

Admire me, caress me, he seemed to say. But do not expect me to reciprocate, for we hardly know each other. A Labrador Retriever I am not.

This was the breed's trademark reserve with strangers, important enough that it is noted

Photo: ThruMarzenasLens.com

twice in the standard. Born of intelligence and a strong sense of self, this reticence to give of themselves to just anyone belies the wickedly funny, cloyingly sweet, rabidly affectionate creatures Ridgebacks can be with those they know and love.

Once you get to know the breed, you see that other side, and find that new level of depth and connection. The awe that I felt that day – What is going on behind those dark brown eyes? Could I handle this big red package of brawn and determination? – has been replaced by a familiarity that is comforting and easy. Like an old married couple, it's automatic and intuitive – with the occasional curve ball thrown in, just to make things interesting.

But I still remember that feeling of newness, of wanting to know everything about this aristocratic and vibrant breed, of not wanting to make a mistake in raising my first one, of wishing I had a Rosetta Stone that would tell me what to expect, what to worry about and what not to.

Of course, this book is not intended to be the locus of all knowledge and information about the Rhodesian Ridgeback breed. There is no one way to do anything, and if there was, the world would be a poorer place for it. Your experiences and opinions may vary from mine, and that's perfectly fine. Above all, hold your breeder's guidance and opinion in high regard: If she is a true breeder, she knows her line and she is an expert on her dogs.

But what this book is, is a breed-specific guide written by someone who knows the breed. (You'd be surprised how many mass-produced breed books aren't.) It is as specific to Ridgebacks as that telltale stripe of hair up their back. It is a celebration and exploration of Ridgebackness, which is so hard to define, but so intuitively obvious to anyone who has taken the time to know and cherish the breed.

This is the book I wish I had when I got my first Ridgeback puppy.

CHAPTER 1

Is the Ridgeback Right for Me?

The key to answering the above question – for any breed, not just the Ridgeback – is to research its origins and history. There, you will find the essence of the breed – the hard-wired traits that may or may not work for your lifestyle. It's one thing to appreciate and admire a breed; it's another to live with it, day in and day out.

Generally speaking, there are two qualities that can make Ridgebacks a challenge to own. The first is the breed's lack of reflexive obedience. This is a thinking breed that will always take its own measure of the situation at hand and will not automatically accept your own assessment as gospel. That doesn't mean that the Ridgeback will always be self-directed, but it does mean that you will have to work more creatively and thoughtfully to get him to respond to your wishes than you would with an "easier" breed.

The second challenge to owning a Ridgeback is its prey drive. Not all Ridgebacks lock in so intensely on a moving target like a squirrel or deer that they will ignore your commands, but many will. Enough so that I tell people who seek out a Ridgeback that they should not acquire the breed with the anticipation that it can be an off-leash dog who responds with a reliable recall. If the gods are kind to you and this is the case, then consider yourself the exception that proves the rule. But if an off-leash lifestyle is a deal-breaker – hikers, take note – this is not the breed for you.

Ridgeback temperament is tricky to describe, because it is a balancing act between the breed's stubbornness and sensitivity. Before I got a Ridgeback, I read all these descriptions of how the breed was difficult to train, how it was not for first-time owners, how it was a powerful dog that required an experienced hand. It sounded intimidating and sort of mystical, like I needed some special cereal-box decoder ring to figure out how to raise and train one of these beautiful brown dogs.

In practice, it wasn't quite that daunting, but it definitely was different from the German Shepherd mixes that I had owned before.

The key to managing a Ridgeback is to remember that you need to be firm and flexible at the same time, sort of like a skyscraper: Strong enough to stand up to the challenges that the dog presents to you, but flexible enough to bend at the right moment so you don't snap.

First, the strength part: You as an owner must be firm and set clear boundaries. Your Ridgeback needs to know you are in charge, and that attempts to distract or charm you are not going to succeed. There is nothing more destabilizing to a Ridgeback than a wishy-washy owner who approaches life with a sense of hesitancy or trepidation. Your Ridgeback excels at reading you and your emotions, and if she thinks you are overwhelmed or unable to lead, she will attempt to take that role over for herself. And, trust me, the decisions she makes will ultimately get you both into a lot of trouble.

Conversely, rigid and autocratic owners are just as bad for a Ridgeback, which brings us to the flexibility part. As far back as people have been writing about Ridgebacks, they have been talking about the breed's sensitive nature. "… Rough treatment … should never be administered to these dogs, especially when they are young," said Francis Barnes, who compiled the first Ridgeback standard in 1922. "They go to pieces with handling of that kind."

Though he is powerful and stubborn, the Ridgeback does not tolerate harsh treatment. He cannot handle the corporal punishment – such as constant collar jerks or "alpha rolls" – that a Sporting dog would just shrug off. The Ridgeback, after all, is a Hound, just like a Saluki or an Afghan Hound: He is sensitive. When confronted with abuse or harsh handling, he either shuts down or escalates his response in an effort to get away. This is not bad temperament: It is mishandling on the part of the owner.

Beneath that tough-guy exterior is a sensitive soul, and Ridgeback owners need to work *with* it, instead of against it. Unlike a Sporting or even Working dog, a Ridgeback will not submit to the will of the human in charge if she thinks the idea is a bad one. This is a breed that needs to be reasoned with. When a Ridgeback who is worried or overwhelmed is forced to comply, that Ridgeback will resist.

Physically overpowering a dog the size of a Ridgeback is not only difficult, but it will erode the trust that is so vital to your relationship. (How do you get him to do what you want? By outsmarting him and letting him think it is his idea. More on that in later chapters. For now, just know that it is more than possible.)

Raising a Ridgeback properly is not too different from raising a child: You need firmness and boundaries, tempered with lots of affection and understanding. The trick is in balancing those extremes: Too much of one, and you get an unruly, egocentric brat. Too much of the other, and you raise a neurotic mess. Meet in the middle.

I probably should have called this chapter "Are You Right for the Ridgeback?" Because, no matter how much you admire them, or how beautiful you think they are, there are certain things about Ridgebacks that are non-negotiable. With that in mind, here are some questions to ask yourself. Be honest with your answers, because in the end you're only fooling yourself.

Do you have a fenced yard – or an exercise plan?

The Ridgeback's great athleticism and intelligence are what attract many of us to the breed. But the intensely prey-driven Ridgeback is not reliable off leash. If a squirrel or other creature crosses her path, your Ridgeback will be off like a shot. Your commands will go unheeded. If there is a two-lane highway between your Ridgeback and the squirrel, well … you can finish the sentence.

If you don't have a fenced yard, then are you committed to walking your dog on leash, or do you have a secure, fenced area where he can run?

If you are an avid hiker or off-road biker whose dream is to have a dog who will accompany you off leash, no matter what wildlife or distractions cross your path, you need to seriously rethink your expectations – or your choice of breed.

Do you have small children?

Let's be really clear on this: As a breed, the Rhodesian Ridgeback is the consummate family dog. Though of course you should never leave any dog of any breed unattended with small children, nor should you allow children to poke, prod or pull any part of a dog, the reality is that Ridgebacks are extremely tolerant of children. Some breeds, when roused or pestered by a toddler, might snap at the object of their annoyance. But the typical Ridgeback response is to get up, shake it off and walk away.

Young Ridgebacks are active and inquisitive.
Photo: Theresa M. Lyons

That said, Ridgebacks are big dogs who can unintentionally send small children scattering like bowling pins. Ridgebacks – in particular, energetic adolescents – play the same way they hunt: chasing, leaping, body-slamming. Ridgeback tails are powerful and, when employed in the expression of happiness, can leave welt marks.

The Ridgeback's natural prey drive can be an issue with very young and small children. If a toddler runs across the room shrieking, the average Ridgeback will chase him, even knock him down. This isn't aggression, it's simply instinct, and when confronted with the sobbing child, the Ridgeback will invariably lick his face and ask what all the fuss is about.

Finally, Ridgeback puppy teeth are needle-sharp, and the natural mouthiness that accompanies teething – again, this is not biting, it is a natural canine imperative – can be trying for parents who envisioned more of a Hallmark-card puppyhood.

For these reasons, many Ridgeback breeders are reluctant to sell puppies to families with children younger than five years. That is more or less the age at which a child is identifiable to the dog as a bona-fide human, not some furless contemporary. Children are simply sturdier at this age, and intellectually able to understand how to handle the dog and not take the vagaries of puppyhood personally.

What other animals do you have?

The Ridgeback's very physical play style isn't just a potential issue with young children. Some breeds – say, Dachshunds or even Greyhounds –might be too fragile and "crunchy" to withstand Ridgeback play sessions. Physical compatibility has less to do with the size of the dog – smaller breeds such as Border Terriers and even Whippets are terrific household companions with Ridgebacks – and more with its sturdiness. A Ridgeback joining an Italian Greyhound household is not something you can contemplate without wincing.

Also, Ridgebacks are often not a good mix with "serious" breeds, such as Akitas and Mastiffs, who demand deference. The Ridgeback's in-your-face physical style and jokester attitude (they think running headlong at you at

Independence is hard-wired in the breed.

Photo: Mary Bloom

25 miles per hour is amusing) might push those breeds to their limits.

When it comes to cats, rabbits and other non-canines, keep in mind that Ridgebacks love to chase. So introducing an adult Ridgeback to a mixed-species household might prove a challenge. You are going to need intense supervision, patience and time to create a peaceable kingdom. In the case of cats, if you have one who is inclined to stand her ground, puff up and hiss at the Ridgeback interloper, that might make things easier: It is the chasing that makes the Ridgeback lose his composure and go into hunting mode.

Usually, a puppy can more easily be "programmed" to accept prey animals in the household than an adult can. Generally speaking, a Ridgeback who has been raised with animals of other species will be inclined to see them as part of his "pack" and will not intentionally harm them. However, just because a Ridgeback doesn't chase "his" cat doesn't mean he won't chase others in a different context.

What kind of trainer are you?

Because he survived on the hunt using his own wits, the Ridgeback is intensely independent. A Ridgeback loves his humans, but he does not need their endless approval. A Ridgeback is not reflexively obedient.

This doesn't mean he is untrainable, but it does mean that he needs short, positive training sessions. He will not sit 10 times in a row simply because you asked him: He will think, after the second or third request, that you are just being stupid.

There are some people who want a very hierarchical relationship with their dog. The Ridgeback will not provide this. He will love you, and he will protect you, but your wish is not his every command. If your ego cannot handle that, do not get a Ridgeback. In the obedience ring, I have completed entire exercises by myself – with my dog looking on from the middle of the ring. You need a sense of humor!

The Ridgeback requires a relationship of trust with his handler. This is a breed that makes decisions for itself: Compulsion is doomed to failure. Instead, the Ridgeback must be reasoned with. He will not do something he thinks is life-threatening or dangerous "just because" you said so. This is also a breed that must be owner-trained. You cannot hand your Ridgeback off to a trainer, or send him to "camp." He responds only to those whom he trusts or likes.

I have seen Ridgebacks who were sent off to "schools" that used electronic collars to "train" their students – and returned as blank-eyed, cowering messes. There are no shortcuts or magic bullets in training any dog, much less a Ridgeback. If you aren't willing to train your Ridgeback yourself – with the help of a trainer or obedience class, fine, but always with you on the other end of the lead – please don't get one.

Are you looking for a "guard dog"?

Many people see the Ridgeback's imposing presence and physique and think he is an aggressive guard dog. Not true. Like most of us, the Ridgeback is reserved with strangers: He saves his effusive displays for those whom he loves. But a Ridgeback with a correct temperament is never suspicious of guests. He accepts them into his home with the same graciousness that his owner does. He assumes that you are decent and honorable unless proven otherwise.

Photo: Margit Louise Sand Nelson

Some people who are drawn to Working dogs see the Ridgeback as an alternative to a Doberman Pinscher or Rottweiler.

Wrong! A Working dog like a Doberman or Rottie will have a much sharper protection response than a Ridgeback, because the former were bred to guard either property or people, or both. Ridgebacks are natural guardians, but that is not their primary purpose. They are reserved with strangers but not naturally distrustful of them, as some protection breeds can be. They assume that someone they meet is innocent until proven guilty. If you get a Ridgeback expecting it to guard like a Doberman, and attempt to incite that protective instinct when the dog doesn't show it, you will be creating a behavioral problem that will end in tragedy for you and, most definitely, the dog.

Many Ridgeback owners are dismayed that their dogs, especially their males, do not "act

protective." That is because they have found no cause to be wary. The Ridgeback is a very intelligent and discriminating companion. If and when he needs to defend you, he will. Otherwise, you can expect his good nature and pack mentality to extend to all those he meets, provided he has been properly and positively socialized.

If you need a tough-guy dog who gives the hairy eyeball to strangers without the slightest provocation, again, please look to another breed.

Are you a soft touch?

Ridgebacks are gluttons, pure and simple. They will eat until they are bursting, and then they will eat some more. You simply have to be able to say no, or you will soon end up with an obese dog. Similarly, if you don't keep all counters free from food, your Ridgeback will soon become an expert "counter surfer," and drive-by chompings of sandwiches and snacks will become commonplace.

Ridgebacks love their comforts. Most will "turn in" around 8 or 9 in the evening. And once they do, it can be difficult to rouse them. Unless, of course, the refrigerator door opens.

Photo: Nicole Leonhart

As for other bad habits, Ridgebacks will develop them if you allow them to. Jumping up on strangers, persistent crotch-sniffing – they'll happen repeatedly unless you intervene. If you don't want your Ridgeback on the couch or in your bed, then don't allow it, not even

Once permitted on the couch, Ridgebacks will be difficult to evict. One deterrent is cheap, by-the-foot plastic carpet runners. Buy an appropriate length at your hardware store, then place upside down on the couch (or bed or your favorite chair) so the pointy plastic "teeth" that are meant to grip the carpet face up. Most Ridgebacks will find it unpleasant – until they figure out how to pull the runner off, or strategically place a pillow over it. *Photo: Denise Flaim*

once. Because once a Ridgeback has been given the green light, it is very difficult to turn it red again.

Do you want to hear some of the good stuff now?

Unlike a Sporting or Herding dog, a Ridgeback is not "on" all the time. Provided he gets enough exercise, he is content to slumber the day away, following you or the shafts of sunlight from room to room – never clingy, but always a tangible presence. He housebreaks easily and is not a career chewer (though, like any dog, he needs to be taught not to teethe on the Chippendale highboy). If given lots of exercise and time with his owner, he can make a suitable apartment dog. He will not, however, tolerate being tied up outside, away from his home and family.

This is arguably the biggest lap dog in the universe. Ridgeback love their creature comforts, and, like canine canaries, they prefer to sleep entirely covered. Unlike many other breeds, they rarely "overheat" when snuggling with you. There is no greater pleasure in this world than curling up on the sofa with your Ridgeback, cheek to cheek, marveling at your good fortune in owning this magnificent, intelligent, intuitive and almost human breed.

Chapter 2

Finding a Breeder

When I got married more than 20 years ago, I went to Kleinfeld to shop for my wedding gown. This was before the Brooklyn store had its own reality show – "Say Yes to the Dress" – but it had long been a legend in bridal circles. If Kleinfeld didn't have it, it pretty much didn't exist.

The selection was overwhelming, but I knew what I was looking for, and, armed with my preferences, the saleswoman waded into the racks of billowy white fabric. The third dress she came out with was it. It met all my criteria, looked great on, and I just knew it was right. But, unnerved by my early success, I insisted on trying on a dozen other dresses. And with each long zip and rustle of silk, I knew that I had already made my decision.

What does any of this have to do with buying a Ridgeback puppy? Everything, in fact.

Buying a puppy isn't a simple business transaction any more than buying a wedding dress is. A breeder is more than just someone from whom you buy a puppy: A breeder is a resource and sounding board for the life of your puppy – and beyond. And, like my dress search, finding *your* breeder (and I use that preposition intentionally) is part good research and part sheer instinct.

First, you need to do your fact-finding so you know what you are looking for, starting with whether not the breed is a good match for you. (See Chapter 1.) Then you need to determine what your specific needs are: Do you plan to compete in lure coursing or agility? Do you want to dabble in showing this puppy? Does your life situation require a certain temperament?

Next, you need to begin your search among a pool of reputable breeders. (Remember, I found my perfect dress with such relative ease because I was starting off with a quality selection.) The best place to do that is among the membership of the breed's recognized parent club. In some countries, such as Germany, dog politics being what they are, there are several such clubs. In the U.S., there is only one: the Rhodesian Ridgeback Club of the United States, or RRCUS (pronounced "ruckus" for short).

Of course, membership in a parent club does not confer instant credibility. There are bad apples in every bunch. But the vast majority of breeders who have taken the time and effort to join their national breed club have done so because they care deeply about the breed and want to be part of its stewardship. The more activities a breeder is involved in, the better: Participating in not just dog shows, but also performance events such as lure coursing and agility, therapy-dog work and initiatives within the breed club all demonstrate that a breeder is committed to the "big picture."

The RRCUS web site at www.rrcus.org offers a breeders' directory that is organized by state. Take the time to browse through various breeders' sites. You'll soon notice that while they are all celebrations of the breeders' own dogs and breeding programs, they are all different in terms of emphasis and tone. One breeder might be very focused on show wins, another on her agility stars. One might make a point of the involvement of her children in helping raise the pups, another on how many years he has been in the breed. Again, there are no "right" answers. Look for the website that "speaks" to you. This is the perception the breeder has of himself, that he wants to broadcast to the world. This doesn't mean that you should be taken in by a slick website – because there are some foolers out there. But, generally speaking, a breeder's website is often a good gauge of what his priorities are.

Once you find one or more breeders to whom you are drawn, you'll have exchanges via email, phone and, eventually, in person that are the puppy buyer's equivalent of the fitting room. Somewhere in that process, you'll come across the right breeder for you, and you will just *know*. Don't underestimate that gut feeling – and don't second-guess it.

'Buying' a Breeder

You've gone to the breed-club web site (in the U.S., www.rrcus.org), found the breeder's directory, spent hours bopping from site to site, and now are more confused than ever. Some dogs are bigger, some smaller; some are deep red and some are almost gold in color; some have a certain head style or body outline. All you want is a reasonably attractive, healthy dog with a good temperament. And most reputable breeders seem to have that.

How, then, do you choose?

When puppy people call me, I tell them that they shouldn't think of this process as buying a puppy. What they are really buying is a *breeder*.

Just like our dogs, breeders are all different. We have different personalities, different approaches to life, different priorities. Your goal should be to find a breeder with whom you connect. Ask yourself, "Could I get along with this person? Would I be comfortable calling her if I was having a crisis with my dog – and do I think she would respond?"

Some breeders may be reputable and conscientious, and have lovely dogs, but if you feel uncomfortable interacting with them, then heed that internal warning. It has nothing to do with that breeder's ethics, and everything to do with your chemistrys.

You are buying a relationship with your breeder for the hopefully long lifetime of your puppy. It has to be a relationship you are comfortable with. Some breeders are very involved in their puppies' lives; others are more reserved. Some have very particular diet and vaccine schedules that they want you to follow; others are more flexible about nutrition and rearing. Nobody's right or wrong; they're just different. I have a breeder-friend whose contract requires her buyers to send her a holiday card with the dog's photo every December. At first I thought this was a bit much, until she explained her logic: That annual card allowed her to check in on the puppy throughout his lifetime, revealing problems both minor (the dog was overweight) and major (the family gave the dog away

Newborn Ridgeback puppies are born without sight or hearing. *Photo: ThruMarzenasLens.com*

and didn't inform her). Some people might find that level of interaction intrusive, while others might be impressed by her commitment. Again, there is no right or wrong – just what is right or wrong for you.

Hallmarks of a Reputable Breeder

• Reputable breeders screen their sires and dams for heritable diseases, many of them performing the tests recommended by the Canine Health Information Center, or CHIC.

• Reputable breeders require you to sign a contract.

• In that contract, reputable breeders require that their pet-quality puppies be spayed or neutered at an appropriate time.

• Reputable breeders also stipulate that should you no longer want your Ridgeback, no matter what his age or the reason, you must return the dog to them.

• Reputable breeders will not hesitate to let you visit and meet their dogs.

• Reputable breeders are likely to try to talk you out of the Ridgeback if they feel you are not a good fit for the breed.

• Reputable breeders do not sell their puppies in public places, nor do they sell individual puppies on online auction or puppy sites.

Where Not to Go

Everyone knows they are supposed to buy a dog from a "reputable breeder," but nonetheless some find themselves buying from less-than-scrupulous sources, including ...

• *Pet stores.* Most buyers know this is a red flag, but sometimes the temptation to get what they want, when they want, proves too strong. Yes, pet-store puppies can be taken home in an instant, and, yes, they are cute. But they are not any cheaper than a puppy from a reputable breeder – and sometimes cost significantly more – and they come with no support system. Beyond that, you know nothing about the temperament, health or soundness of the parents. And the likelihood is that your puppy was raised in a high-volume commercial facility – a nice way of saying "puppymill" – with minimal human interaction. That's hardly the best start in life.

A slick website and cute photos are nice, but there's nothing like an in-person visit with your future breeder. *Photo: ThruMarzenasLens.com*

• *Internet dealers.* These "virtual" storefronts are oftentimes no better than brick-and-mortar pet stores, and often their stock comes from high-volume puppymills as well. You are buying "blind" here, too.

• *"Backyard breeders."* This derogatory term refers to casual breeders who have no in-depth breeding knowledge, but who decide to "try their hand" at breeding by putting together two pedigreed Ridgebacks. While backyard-bred puppies can be raised in a loving environment (or not – many such litters are relegated to the garage or basement), you again do not have a lifetime resource should anything come up.

Getting the Timing Right

Most people start looking for a puppy only a few months before they want to acquire one. But, ideally, try to start at least six months, preferably a year, before your target date of bringing a puppy home. Many female Ridgebacks cycle every eight to 12 months, which means there is often a wait for litters. And having a long lead time gives you a leisurely opportunity to meet breeders and make an intelligent decision without the emotional tug of a newly born litter. A breeder does not have to have puppies on the ground for you to call and say, "I am interested in the breed. May I come and meet your dogs?"

Every breeder's philosophy is different. Here is mine: There tend to be two types of puppy buyers – those who want to buy from a particular breeder because they have fallen for her and her dogs, and those for whom timing is the most important criterion. The former are not necessarily better than the latter: Schoolteachers, for example, invariably want puppies born in spring so they can devote their summer vacation to welcoming them to the household.

I prefer to meet puppy buyers before the litter arrives – if possible, even before the breeding takes place. Getting together in person lets you meet and interact with my dogs. And it permits both of us to decide if we are "right" for each other. But that doesn't mean "drop-ins" aren't welcome: It seems that in every litter, there is a last-minute cancellation because of unforeseen circumstances – like a sudden layoff or illness in the family. But if you are the type of person who wants to be reasonably assured of a puppy – rather than gliding along on serendipity, which can produce wonderful, unexpected opportunities, if you are flexible – then planning as far ahead as possible will likely work best for you.

The best way to acquire a puppy is to plan for one as much as a year in advance. But for those who are willing to rely on serendipity, the universe has a way of providing.
Photo: Pat Hoffmann

Where the Dogs Are

The gleaming red dogs, their laser-focused handlers, the stern judges – at first glance, dog shows can seem intimidating.

But for a prospective Ridgeback owner, there is no better starting point for research. Dog shows aren't just beauty pageants. When a judge awards a ribbon, he or she signifies that the recipient is a good representation of the breed – and might deserve to be bred. This is precisely why many reputable Ridgeback breeders show their dogs: to get an objective evaluation of their breeding program.

Breeders are strictly prohibited from selling puppies at dog shows, anywhere on the grounds. Still, a show is a great place to introduce yourself, chat about the breeder's dogs, inquire about future litters and – of course – admire a whole bunch of beautiful Ridgebacks.

To newcomers, dog shows can seem like a closed culture where everyone is an "insider" but you. The best antidote is to be prepared and know some basic etiquette. Here are some tips to get you on your way:

Find the action. To locate a dog show, visit www.infodog.com. Click on "Show Information," then "Show Calendar" or "Search by State." (Amid the listings, look for "AB," which stands for all-breed show.) Several days before the show, find it on Infodog again, and select "Judging Program." This will tell you how many Ridgebacks are entered, their ring number, and the time they will be judged.

Nearby shows can be fruitful because you have a good chance that some of the breeders will be local.

If it is geographically feasible, try to go to a benched show, which requires dogs to stay on the premises all day so they can be seen by the public. Once commonplace, today only a handful of benched shows remain. While New York's Westminster is the most famous, others include Philadelphia, Chicago and San Francisco.

Buy a catalog. Your first stop on the show grounds should be the table where show catalogs are sold. An invaluable reference tool, the catalog contains the ownership and breeder information of every dog entered. Each dog is assigned a number, which his handler wears on an armband.

Observe the dogs' temperaments. How are they handling the situation? Which ones do you want to approach – and can you approach them? Circle those and star them.

Timing is everything. When's the best time to engage a sky diver in conversation – before or after he jumps? While showing dogs isn't like hurtling out of an airplane, most handlers are steadying their nerves and readying their dogs before they enter the ring.

The optimal time to introduce yourself is after the showing is over, although it's important to remember that the breed winners stay on for further competition and many of the losers will be in a rush for the door.

Use your judgment: An exhibitor who looks flustered or distracted isn't a candidate for a heart to heart. For others, "Do you have a minute to talk?" is a good ice-breaker. And while Ridgebacks are "wash and wear" dogs whose coifs don't get mussed with a hearty hello pat, always ask permission before petting a dog.

Follow-up at home. Most Ridgebacks tend to be more reserved and standoffish at dog shows: There is a lot to grab their attention, and passersby petting them may not get more than a fleeting tail wag. The best place to really see Ridgeback temperament is at home, when they can focus on you, and, on familiar terrain, show you their funny and laidback side. If you connect with one or two breeders at the show, be sure to schedule some time to visit with them at their homes to see this important "flip side." Otherwise, it is easy to think that the "staring statue" persona that Ridgebacks sometimes present at ringside is who they really are, and nothing could be further from the truth!

Photo: Theresa M. Lyons

Buying Etiquette

Understandably, if you are anxious to cement your reservation for a puppy, you might want to keep as many options open as possible. But whatever you do, do not sit on two waiting lists at once, unless both breeders are aware that you are doing so.

When a breeder has a litter, she is very careful not to overbook, because there is nothing worse than disappointing someone. So, when her list is full, with one person per puppy, she begins to turn away buyers. If you say you want a puppy, but then drop off the list to pursue something "better," then you are being inconsiderate, to say the least.

To avoid this, some breeders take deposits before the litter is born, or almost immediately after. I personally don't like to do this, because I don't want the fear of losing a deposit to be the primary thing holding someone to purchasing one of my puppies. Also, what if the litter is smaller than I anticipated, or I have mostly boys and everyone on my list wants girls? I do keep a waiting list, check in with everyone after the puppies are born to determine if their needs and preferences are still the same, and typically take a deposit around three weeks; by this time, the puppies are close to being weaned and those precarious first few weeks are behind us.

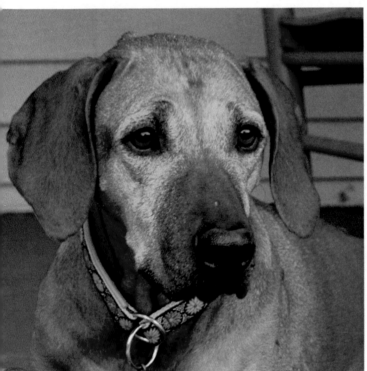

Every reputable breeder sets out with the intention of breeding Ridgebacks who will live long, healthy lives.

Photo: Denise Flaim

If you do find yourself in a struggle over whether to commit to Breeder A or Breeder B, honesty is the best policy. Breeders tend to talk to one another – unless they don't get along, which happens, too – and you'd be surprised at how often "list squatters" are outed. Often what happens is that then neither breeder wants to deal with you, because you've been disingenuous.

Breeders appreciate forthrightness, and they understand if you might be temporarily up in the air about a particular litter, and might need to formulate a back-up plan. Consider this explanation, for example: "I am on the waiting list for Breeder X's current litter, which is six weeks old. I have my heart set on a female, and in this litter there are only two. One has already been promised, and Breeder X is not sure if she is keeping the other female. If she doesn't, then I will get her. But if she does, then I will be without a puppy, and Breeder X doesn't anticipate having another litter for 18 months or so. I am writing to inquire about whether you have any room on the list for your upcoming litter – I would love to be considered for a puppy if this little girl with Breeder X doesn't work out."

Most breeders would be happy to work with such an upfront buyer – and most would also contact Breeder X to see if the story is legitimate, and to see if she would have any objections to proceeding as our fictional buyer suggests.

Another etiquette item: Many initial communications with breeders are done via email, a medium which lacks the ability to clearly convey the writer's tone, as well as humor and nuance. Nothing is more off putting to a breeder than to receive a "form letter" that has clearly been sent to every other breeder in that state or locality. Or to receive a curt email that asks, simply, "Do you have puppies, and how much?"

When I get an email from a prospective buyer, I am pleased when it shows that the writer has taken as much time to learn about me and my dogs as I am about to take in talking to her about the possibility of a puppy. The best emails say the prospective buyers have been to my website and read a bit about me and my dogs; tell me in turn something about themselves, their family, where they live, what their dog experience is; talk a bit about why they want a Ridgeback, and, finally, ask if there is a convenient time to speak or visit.

If you have in-depth questions, save them for that conversation. And that goes for questions about price. When people ask a breeder how much a puppy is, it's usually because they honestly have no idea and want to be sure they have the resources to purchase one. But this kind of query can be misinterpreted, especially if it is among the first questions you ask.

Another Option: Rescue

This book is called "Your Rhodesian Ridgeback Puppy," and that last word is its focus. But you should be aware of Rhodesian Ridgeback Rescue as an option for a wonderful purebred companion – maybe for a sidekick for your grown puppy when the time comes.

Purebred Ridgeback puppies in rescue are not common: Most of the dogs being rehomed by the group are adolescents and adults. That's simply because puppies are easy to give away and place – even if, sadly, the new owners are as ill equipped to give them a good home as the first.

Rhodesian Ridgeback Rescue (www.ridgebackrescue.org) is an all-volunteer organization run by experienced Ridgeback people who know the breed and can help you make a good match. Many will foster a rescue in their home along with their own dogs to really assess the dog's temperament and level of socialization. Even if you don't end up adopting from them, consider a donation so they can continue their important work.

Chapter 3

10 Questions to Ask a Ridgeback Breeder

When you finally get a chance to talk to or visit with a breeder, you likely will have dozens of questions. It's perfectly fine to write them down, so you don't forget them. Try to do your research in advance, so you aren't taking up time asking basic questions – like "What is a dermoid sinus?" "What makes a dog pet quality?" – that you could be researching in advance. (And which you'll find the answers to later in this book.) Instead, use your time to ask questions that will give you insight into how this particular breeder approaches the breed, and her opinions about topics where there is a divergence of opinion among her peers, such as what age to spay-neuter, what to feed or how to vaccinate.

Here are 10 questions you might consider asking.

1. Why did you do this breeding?

Reputable Rhodesian Ridgeback breeders do not just put two dogs together in order to make more dogs. Instead, they pair dogs so that each one's strength compensate for the other's weaknesses. A good breeder should be able to articulate the "why" behind a particular pairing – and how she expects the litter to be an improvement on both parents.

Why does this matter if you "only want a pet"? Because if a breeder does not breed for the correct look or temperament of a dog, then his or her dogs eventually will drift away from what the breed is supposed to look and act like. And even if the pedigree papers say a dog is a Rhodesian Ridgeback, what does that matter if the dog doesn't look or act anything like the breed to which he belongs?

2. Do you have a mandatory return-to-breeder clause in your contract in the event the puppy buyer no longer wants the dog – at any age, no questions asked?

Reputable breeders of any breed require all unwanted dogs of their breeding to be returned to them, and reputable Rhodesian Ridgeback breeders are no different. In this day and age, when shelters are overrun with abandoned dogs, breeders must not add to the overpopulation problem.

3. Do you sell your pet-quality puppies on mandatory spay-neuter contracts?

Reputable Ridgeback breeders require pet-quality dogs to be spayed or neutered at an appropriate age (which can vary quite a bit, depending on the breeder – we'll discuss that in a later chapter). In the U.S., reputable breeders often will sell such dogs on a "limited registration": This means that the Ridgeback is registered with the American Kennel Club, and she can be entered in all AKC events except conformation shows. Also, any puppies resulting from the breeding of a limited-registration dog can't be AKC registered.

4. What registry are you using?

The American Kennel Club (AKC) and United Kennel Club (UKC) are reputable registries – they have a "family tree" of dogs going back dozens of generations. Only the offspring of registered dogs can be registered themselves. These registries also offer DNA testing to check parentage. In this way, buyers are assured that what is on the pedigree is correct – that the sire is indeed the sire and the dam is the dam.

Several years ago, when the AKC began to require submission of DNA on frequently used sires and when it increased inspections of kennels, many commercial breeders just left and started their own registries. These registries bank on the fact that buyers expect "papers," but do not bother to see what the acronym on them really is. Many will register any dog, as long as you provide a name and a check – resulting in a pedigree that is often not worth the paper it is printed on.

5. Can I meet the puppies' mother (or, sometimes, father)?

At first glance, having the sire on premise may seem like a good thing, because, after all, it is wonderful to meet both your puppy's parents and gauge their well-being and temperament. Keep in mind, however, that a reputable breeder is looking for the perfect match for his female. That may not necessarily be the stud dog that lives under his roof. Those breeders who use stud dogs that are out of state or clear across the country are doing so despite the inconvenience and extra cost because they are going the extra mile to plan a breeding that they believe will have the best chances of accomplishing their goals.

So in many cases, the stud will not be on premise. But the breeder should be able to show you photographs of him, share the results of his health screenings, and articulate why she chose him to complement her female.

In most cases, the mother of the puppies will be present. While she should be protective of her litter, she should have a stable temperament and be reasonably tolerant of your presence. Note the conditions in which the puppies are kept: Whether in a private home or a kennel, the surroundings should be clean and sanitary.

There are, however, some legitimate scenarios in which the dam is not present:

• **Stud-fee puppies.** Sometimes, in lieu of a stud fee, a stud-dog owner will request a puppy. Such puppies are generally show quality, and the stud-dog owner may choose to bring the puppy home and sell him to a local buyer if there is no room at her place for another dog. Such arrangements are very common. The stud-dog owner should be willing to share photographs of the dam, as well as contact information for the breeder of record. And you will of course be able to meet the stud dog.

• **Co-ownerships.** Because many breeders run small, home-based operations, as opposed to having kennel facilities, some choose to place their females on co-ownerships. When they work out, these are win-win arrangements: The breeder can have access to a female

A breeder's whelping box should be set up in a quiet, private area. *Photo: ThruMarzenasLens.com*

in order to show and breed her, and can maintain a relatively vibrant breeding program without overwhelming herself with a growing number of dogs under one roof. And the dog benefits because she has a loving home with doting owners in which she gets all the attention and love she deserves.

In such situations, the dam may not be on the premises when you first visit, as the litter may be whelped at the co-owner's home. If the litter is whelped at the breeder's, the dam might go back home after the puppies are weaned, especially if there is an older female at the breeder's home who can take over "mommy duty" and teach the puppies correct manners and good inter-doggie coping skills.

In both of these scenarios, the breeder should be able to explain the arrangements that led to the breeding and whelping, and, unless the dam is out of state, arrange for you to meet her, either at her home or during a pre-scheduled visit.

6. What health screenings have you done?

The Rhodesian Ridgeback is a generally healthy breed, and reputable breeders perform a variety of health tests to ensure that it stays that way. Though the Rhodesian Ridgeback Club of the United States (RRCUS) requires member breeders to breed only those dogs that pass orthopedic tests that prove they do not have elbow or hip dysplasia, many breeders do not stop there, often testing eyes, hearts and thyroids as well. The Orthopedic Foundation for Animals (www.offa.org) and the Canine Health Information Center, or

CHIC (www.caninehealthinfo.org), list health screenings for individual dogs.

In other parts of the world, different health tests are mandated. Hip screening has become an increasingly widespread breeding requirement around the globe.

7. How are your puppies raised?

Some breeders make a big deal of the fact that their litters are raised in their homes, and, in fact, this can be a huge plus, as those puppies benefit from frequent interaction with family members and the daily traffic of a busy household. But this doesn't mean that reputable breeders who operate small-scale hobby kennels are a less desirable option.

Toys designed for human toddlers, like the sit-and-spin pictured here, give puppies a chance to experiment with new sounds and shifting footing. *Photo: Denise Flaim*

Reputable Ridgeback breeders do not sell their puppies before eight weeks of age, and before that time they ensure that these new canine souls get as much socialization and positive reinforcement as possible. As much as a specific environment in which a puppy is raised, you are looking for interaction. Are the puppies handled frequently? Do they have the opportunity to see and interact with other people and dogs? Where do they spend the majority of their time? Does the breeder do any early neurological stimulation, which helps build a dog's mental stability and flexibility?

In other words: Is this an enriching environment?

8. Do you show your dogs?

Not all reputable breeders show their dogs, and not all dog-show breeders are necessarily reputable. But involvement in dog shows – which by definition is a way to determine if a given dog is good enough to be bred – shows a commitment to the breed. If the breeder doesn't show her dogs, does she compete with them in any other venue, such as agility, obedience or lure coursing?

9. Do you belong to the Rhodesian Ridgeback parent club, or any other dog clubs?

Ideally, a Ridgeback breeder should belong to the parent club of the country in which she resides. Parent clubs keep breeders aware of developments in the breed, and health research and initiatives, as well as provide an annual forum, in the form of a "national specialty" or "club show," for breeders to convene and compare breeding stock.

That said, like all clubs, parent clubs are not immune to politics, and some breeders may have valid reasons for not being members. Nonetheless, a breeder should belong to some type of dog-related club, whether it is a performance organization such as an agility or lure-coursing club, or a local all-breed club. No Rhodesian Ridgeback breeder should exist, or breed, in a vacuum: Breeders need the support and input of their peers to grow as good dog people.

10. How long have you been involved in Ridgebacks?

A long tenure doesn't necessarily translate into a good breeder: Bad breeders can have longevity, too. But there is no substitute for experience, and you need to feel assured that your breeder is someone you can turn to if you need help or guidance. Newer breeders often have mentors who themselves have been breeding Rhodesian Ridgebacks for decades, and in this way, you can benefit from their length and breadth of experience as well.

Talking Money

You'll notice that I didn't put the question, "How much is one of your puppies?" on my top 10 list. It's not that the question is unimportant. It's just that it shouldn't be one of the most important questions you ask.

What is behind the price of a properly bred purebred Ridgeback? Quite a bit, including:

Health screenings. As I said earlier, the Rhodesian Ridgeback Club of the United States requires in its code of ethics that breeders screen their dogs for hip and elbow dysplasia. Depending on geography, this can cost between $300 and $1,000. But many breeders do many more tests than that, including eye, thyroid and cardiac screenings, as well as DNA tests for degenerative myelopathy and heritable deafness.

Show fees. If at all possible, breeders try to obtain championships on their breeding stock.

It not only serves as independent validation that their dogs meet the breed standard, but it allows them to compare their dogs to those of their fellow breeders, and can oftentimes raise the bar in their breeding program. But, depending on a number of factors – including the experience level of the dog and handler – this can take some time. Expenses include entry fees, mileage and travel costs.

Stud Fees. Love isn't cheap, especially when it comes to finding a sire for a litter. Stud fees are roughly equivalent to the price of a pet-quality puppy. Depending on location, that can range from $700 to $2,000 – sometimes more if the male in question is an exceptionally good producer or a celebrated winner. If no puppies result, there usually is no refund; oftentimes, just a "return of service," or free repeat breeding, is offered instead.

When it comes to finding the right stud dog, breeders often go long distances, either by driving for days or flying their female to the stud dog. If a stud-dog owner has to keep the female for an extended period, he might charge a handling or boarding fee.

Thanks to technology, problems with conflicting schedules or daunting distances can be solved with artificial insemination. With "fresh extended" or "chilled" semen, the dog's sperm is collected by a vet, who then ships it. That additional cost can number in the hundreds of dollars.

Freezing semen has become a popular way of ensuring that a stud dog can be used long after his death. In addition to the regular stud fee, it is customary for the dam owner to pay for packaging and shipment of the frozen semen, as well as surgical implantation.

Add to all that the cost of vaginal smears and daily progesterone tests to track the dam's hormone levels, as well as an emergency Caesarian section if labor does not go as planned, and the cost of the simple act of procreation can easily reach the thousands.

Puppy patrol. Caring for puppies isn't just exhausting: It's expensive. Vet visits for health checks, worming, dewclaw removal (if the breeder opts to remove these front claws, which is common in the U.S., but not abroad) and inoculations add up quickly. Good nutrition also doesn't come cheap. Many Ridgeback breeders wean their puppies onto human-grade food, or high-end commercial dog food.

While vet bills and grocery-store receipts are easy to tabulate, it's far more difficult to put a price on the intense interaction and socialization that a good breeder gives her pups, starting at birth.

Like many large-breed dogs, Ridgeback dams can suffocate newborn puppies by lying on or rolling over on them. As a result, many breeders sleep beside the whelping box for the first two weeks, essentially monitoring the litter around the clock with baby monitors and intercoms to make sure no one is in distress.

Screening prospective owners is another huge time commitment. Many breeders require new owners to visit, often long before the puppies are born.

The big picture. In some sense, the cost of a litter never ends – because neither does the reputable breeder's quest for knowledge.

After decades of seeking out mentors and studying her breed, a breeder often becomes so knowledgeable that she becomes a mentor herself – investing time and resources to teach newcomers what the "old-timers" taught her.

From an accounting perspective, it is a losing proposition. But committed breeders never stop to consider the lopsided math.

Why breed? Breeders might just as well as themselves "Why walk?" or "Why breathe?" Because it's a passion. And if it isn't, they shouldn't be doing it.

Where in the world ... ? Finally, the cost of a puppy is heavily dependent on geography. Breeders in major metropolitan areas like Los Angeles or New York charge more for their pet puppies (as much as $2,500) because of their high overhead – including veterinary care and general cost of living. By contrast, in a more rural area, you might pay less than $1,000.

Some Ridgebacks are born without ridges, and prices for these ridgeless puppies can differ dramatically. Some breeders charge as much for them as they do their ridged siblings. Others sell them for just the cost of rearing, $500 or $700.

The difference likely has to do with the perception shift regarding ridgeless puppies in the breed. As recently as 20 years ago, ridgeless puppies were routinely euthanized, so when more progressive breeders began to rear them and sell them as pets, they felt somewhat

The "puppy pile." *Photo: Mary Bloom*

A new life, full of promise. Good breeders try to maximize a puppy's odds of success.
Photo: ThruMarzenasLens.com

chagrinned about making a profit. More recently, other breeders have made the argument that they put as much care and effort into rearing their ridgeless puppies as their ridged ones, and charging significantly less reinforces the stereotype of them being somehow inferior, which is hardly the case: Sometimes a ridgeless puppy may be the most beautiful and soundest puppy in the litter.

The Bottom Line

Every Rhodesian Ridgeback puppy buyer wants the same thing: a healthy, long-lived puppy with a great temperament. And every Ridgeback breeder has that goal, too: No one sets out to produce sickly, short-lived, ill-tempered dogs.

But there is one powerful variable to contend with in this scenario: Mother Nature.

In the early 2000s, the well-respected canine geneticist Dr. George Padgett, DVM, calculated that the average Rhodesian Ridgeback carries genes for 6.6 genetic defects that have been identified in the breed – about the same number as humans. In other words, every Ridgeback – in fact, every dog – is at risk for producing genetic defects. Like a card game, it just depends what hand you are dealt. One of the reasons breeders perform health tests is to make sure that the dogs we breed do not have any of the disease we are trying to avoid, but that does not mean they will not produce them in their offspring.

Luckily, some health problems have DNA tests that allow breeders, with a simple cheek swab or blood test, to determine whether their dog is a carrier; in many cases, the breeder can simply breed that dog to a non-carrier to ensure that none of the puppies is affected with the disease. In Ridgebacks, there are tests for degenerative myelopathy (a devastating late-onset neurological disorder) and heritable deafness.

But having those tests can be problematic, too: Many breeders, wanting to be conscientious, will avoid breeding to carriers, skewing the gene pool in favor of non-carrier dogs. And what that often will do is inadvertently build up the frequency of another problem, sometimes worse than the one initially being avoided – and usually one for which no test is yet available.

What's the point of all this? To explain to you that in breeding dogs, unfortunately, there are no guarantees. It is sort of like a poker game: Skillful and experienced breeders make educated guesses about what cards will be dealt to them, and strategize to ensure they get the

The cost of rearing a litter, and by extension the price of a puppy, can vary depending on geography.

Photo: ThruMarzenasLens.com

best hand possible. Occasionally, luck decides to act like anything but a lady, and a breeder is dealt a bad hand. Then, she must make the complex calculation of deciding which cards to discard, which to keep – and whether to fold altogether.

The good news is that when the deck is reshuffled, the odds can again tilt in your favor. Just when things seem most disheartening, out pops a royal flush – and renewed incentive to remain at the table and see what the next hand brings.

Like a high-stakes card game, successful breeding requires a lot of skill and knowledge – and not a little amount of luck. Because we are dealing with living, breathing creatures, breeders cannot guarantee outcomes. We can only guarantee that we have done our level best to produce as optimal an outcome as possible. And should something unfortunate happen, the reputable breeder will be at your side to help with advice, experience and resources so you can find the very best solution to any problems at hand.

Chapter 4

Selecting Your Puppy

The long-awaited day has come: The puppies have turned eight weeks old, and it is time to pick up yours. You arrive at the breeder's home, where the puppies are romping on an emerald-green lawn. One puppy looks up from the furry mob and sees you. Entranced, he trots, in slow motion, over to you. You drop to your knees, and he leaps into your lap. You scoop him in your arms and he joyously licks your face. You have found each other – kismet.

Now that we've got that out of your system, let's look at how this process really happens.

If you've done your homework and found a reputable breeder, she is breeding this litter for a reason – usually to produce more breeding stock or performance prospects. That has to be her first focus. It isn't that these puppies are "better" than the one you will end up with – just that they are better suited for the purpose for which she needs them. Indeed, many Ridgeback breeders will tell you that their puppies born without ridges are often the most beautiful and structurally sound in their litters. But because of the requirements of the standard, they are not bred and are placed in pet homes.

When you first talk to a breeder about getting a puppy, she will want to know if you have any specific requirements: Do you want a male or a female? Does the dog you buy need to have a ridge? (Some prospective owners are adamant about this, others could simply care less.) Do you have a preference for nose color? Do you plan to compete with your Ridgeback in performance events such as agility or lure coursing? Do you have children? Are you open to the idea of showing?

Puppy buyers sometimes add other criteria to the list, particularly specific physical attributes: "I want a big, red male with a black mask and a huge head" is a refrain that Ridgeback breeders hear quite a bit – it is, to be honest, the newbie-owner cliché. So is: "I want a show-quality dog, but I don't want to show it."

Oftentimes, what these buyers mean is that they want a puppy that is of good quality, or a puppy that has a good ridge. None of these necessarily translates into a "show dog."

"Pet puppies" typically have a cosmetic feature that precludes them from being shown. Or the puppy might technically be "showable" – that is, she has an acceptable ridge and looks like a Ridgeback – but those are hardly the only criteria. And everything is relative: In a litter that happens to have many high-quality puppies, a breeder might let a puppy go as a pet that in another, more average litter might be one of the show prospects. After all, "pick of the litter" refers to that specific litter, and every litter – even a disappointing one, from the breeder's perspective – has its "pick."

Show puppies are, more realistically, show *potential* puppies, as some do not grow into their promise and turn out to be pets in the end. The one thing breeders do not have is a crystal ball – instead, we have to rely on our experience, our eye, our knowledge of the line and perennially crossed fingers.

Pet vs. Show Quality

In Ridgebacks there are several cosmetic factors evident at birth that eliminate a puppy's show potential. Others appear later on, as the puppies are weaned and develop.

Here is a list, in rough chronological order, of some of the qualities that make a Ridgeback a "pet." As you can see, there are many of them, and most have no impact on a puppy's health, happiness or quality of life.

Ridge – or Lack Thereof

Once a newborn has been whelped and determined to be viable, one of the first things a breeder does is check to see if there is a ridge. If there isn't, that puppy is a pet.

Because ridgelessness is a disqualifying fault in the AKC standard, ridgeless Ridgebacks cannot compete in events where they can earn a championship prefix – specifically, in the conformation ring and on the lure-coursing field. Ridgeless Ridgebacks can, however, participate in all other AKC events, including agility, obedience and tracking. They can also compete in lure-coursing (single stake), oval-tracking and straight racing with the American Sighthound Field Association (ASFA), National Oval Track Racing Association (NOTRA) and the Large Gazehound Racing Association (LGRA), respectively.

Back to our newborn puppy: If there is a ridge, then the breeder looks to see if it is a "show ridge." The Ridgeback standard says the ridge "should contain two identical crowns (whorls) directly opposite each other." A puppy whose ridge has more or less than two crowns, or swirls of hair, is a pet.

If the puppy's ridge has two crowns, then the breeder checks to see if they are more or less symmetrical. If it appears that at maturity the crowns will be offset from each other by more than a half-inch or so … he's a pet. (Outside North America, where breeders tend to be real sticklers about ridges, crowns that are even slightly offset are not shown or bred from. Americans tend to be more forgiving about these non-functional elements.)

If the crowns extend more than a third of the way down the ridge (not very common these days, as the ridge has become more standardized) – again, a pet. Finally, if the ridge is too short, appearing to be more like a comma than a stripe, that puppy is a pet, too.

At birth, the ridge appears very distinctly, and the breeder can get a good sense of how many crowns there are, and where they are placed. After a few days, the incoming fuzzy puppy coat makes the ridge very indistinct for several weeks.

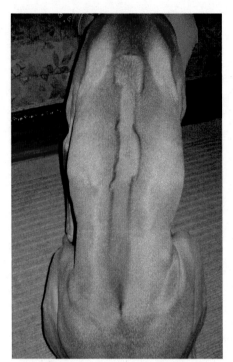

A multi-crown ridge on a pet puppy.
Photo: Denise Flaim

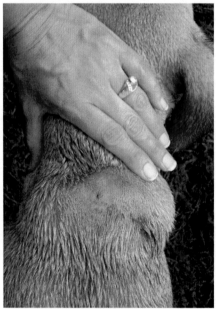

An abscessed dermoid on an adult. The dot in the middle of the shaved area is the opening of the dermoid. The lump to the right is infection. This dermoid was successfully removed.
Photo: Belinda Ruiz Kuchek

That said, the ridge a Ridgeback is born with is the ridge he will have for life. Ridges do not "grow in." They also do not appear and disappear. The hair on the ridge very clearly grows in the opposite direction from the rest of the coat. It is always present. Dogs that periodically get raised hair on their backs and necks are demonstrating hackling, which is common in all dogs; this is not to be confused with a ridge.

Dermoid Sinus

Occasionally, Ridgeback puppies are born with a congenital defect called a dermoid sinus, which can be palpated for at birth. Think of the dermoid sinus as a hollow strand of spaghetti: One end opens up onto the skin, and the other terminates somewhere beneath. (Just how far below it extends and whether it is involved in the spine determines whether the dermoid can be successfully removed with a simple surgery.) The dermoid is lined with skin and hair, which will shed within the narrow tube and cause an infection and, eventually, an abscess.

Some breeders choose to have surgery on dermoid puppies; others decide to euthanize them. The size of the litter, availability of a knowledgeable surgeon and the breeder's previous experiences with dermoid surgeries all factor into the decision. Many breeders whose dermoid puppies successfully heal from surgery sell them for the cost of surgery.

Puppy buyers are understandably concerned about dermoid sinus because it appears in all the literature on the breed. But because this condition is present at birth, it is usually identified by the breeder. Unhappy buyers who find their puppy has a dermoid – often when he is much older and has a grapefruit-sized lump on his neck – usually made the mistake of buying from an inexperienced "backyard" breeder or, worse, a pet store. (The Ridgeback in the photo left was adopted from Craigslist.)

Sometimes, if the person palpating is not experienced, the normal, slightly stringy connective tissue under the skin is mistaken for a dermoid (though it runs parallel to the surface of the skin, not perpendicular to it, as a dermoid does). In the breed's early years, some breeders euthanized whole litters of puppies thinking they had dermoids, only to find that what they were feeling were the slight areas of inflammation left after the puppies' first vaccinations. (For this reason, always have your Ridgeback puppy vaccinated on the flank, *not* on the neck, where the injection site might be mistaken for a dermoid. Don't assume your vet will know this: Tell him or her.)

If there is ever a doubt about whether a dermoid is present, the area can be shaved. The opening of the dermoid will be visible, as a tiny dot. And if the skin is lifted, the skin will pucker inward, because the dermoid will anchor it.

Dermoids can appear on the tail, though they can be hard to palpate and detect. Some dermoids on the tail do not have a visible exit point onto the skin, and so bacteria cannot enter and cause infection. These dermoids often can be left untreated and will not cause a problem for the life of the dog; overzealous surgeons who want to remove such self-contained tail dermoids run the risk of causing neurological damage that could have been avoided by leaving well enough alone.

Dermoid rates vary quite a bit from line to line; some breeders get them regularly while others produce them rarely, if ever. Some breeders – and I am among them – believe that regular supplementation with folic acid measurably reduces dermoid rates. Estimates across the breed worldwide put the dermoid rate in the breed at 4 percent, though, as I've noted, this can vary depending on the line.

Dermoid surgery can be done as early as three days. The older the puppy, the more complicated the surgery.

Excess White

The Ridgeback standard says: "A little white on the chest and toes permissible but excessive white there, on the belly or above the toes is undesirable." But breeders have different

The male puppy at right might have more "paint" on his paws than some breeders would prefer. An American breeder might nonetheless consider him show quality; elsewhere in the world, he would most definitely be a pet. *Photo: Denise Flaim*

A earlier, leggier ancestor of the modern Bulldog was used to develop the Ridgeback. The Bulldog contributed a strong jaw and tenacity, but he also introduced excess white and the kinked tail. *Photo: Dreamstime*

interpretations of how much white is too much white on a Ridgeback.

In Europe and Australia, very little excess white is tolerated. By contrast, many American breeders are more flexible, and will not exclude an exceptional puppy with a short white sock or a white stripe up the neck from the show ring.

Puppies with a great deal of white, particularly on the legs, are often sold as pets, no matter where they live. This is a purely aesthetic consideration, and many owners like the extra white, as it is "flashy." White tends to diminish and fill in with age, so puppies will never have more white than what they are born with, and, oftentimes, end up with less.

Kinked Tail

The Ridgeback is a great cocktail of a dog, resulting from the artful merging of many breeds. One of them was the Bulldog – not the squat, lumbering creature that we know today, but his leggier, more athletic 19th Century ancestor.

The Bulldog contributed a strong holding jaw and general athleticism to the Ridgeback, but he also brought along one undesirable trait: the "dud" or bob tail. We see the vestiges of this today in the occasional puppy born with a kinked tail. Such puppies are not bred because the fault is highly heritable: Breed authority Major Tom Hawley called it "as tenacious as old mamma bulldog herself."

A kink is a bend in the tail caused by a malformation of the spinal vertebrae. It can occur anywhere on the tail – at the very tip, where it will be hardly noticeable, or in the middle, where it can cause the tail to change direction, like an "L"-shaped elbow joint in a pipe. Kinks that occur at the base of the tail may not be noticeable, but for the fact that the dog can't raise her tail!

Very rarely, a kinked tail will interfere with the puppy's ability to relieve himself, and will need to be amputated, or docked, but this will be noted long before the puppy goes to his new home. Usually, though, a kinked tail is simply an aesthetic consideration, and does not detract one bit from a puppy's quality of life or lovability.

Incorrect Bite

By three weeks, puppy teeth begin to emerge and a breeder can begin to see if they will form the correct bite required for the breed, which is a scissors bite.

In a scissors bite, the canines, or fangs, mesh together like their namesake scissor, with the bottom canines fitting neatly in front of the uppers. The front teeth between those canines, the incisors, also mesh perfectly, with the lower incisors resting just inside the uppers.

The most common "off" bite seen in Ridgebacks is an overbite. In this bite, the upper jaw is longer than the lower, and the lower canines are set back further, so that they cannot "lock" into the uppers.

Some veterinarians will panic clients by insisting that overbites need to be corrected, either by pulling teeth or other

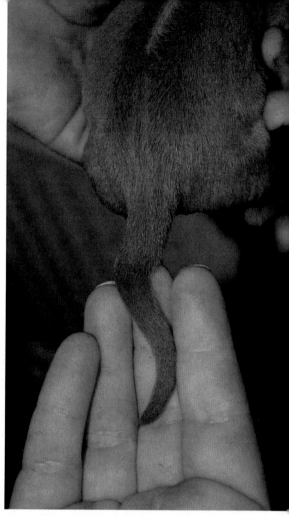

Above: Kinked tail in a newborn. Below: Overbite.
Photos: Theresa M. Lyons and Dreamstime/Anke van Wyck

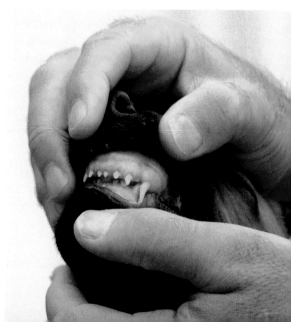

expensive surgery, because the misplaced lower canines will perforate the roof of the mouth. In truth, the vast majority of Ridgebacks with overbites get on perfectly and do not need any veterinary intervention.

Outside of North America, many countries require Ridgebacks used for breeding to have "complete dentition," a fancy way of saying that they have all 42 teeth. This is rarely if ever even a deal-breaker for American breeders.

Male vs. Female

This section could be titled "Chocolate vs. Vanilla," because the two sexes are so different – but equally as delicious.

Male Ridgebacks are on average 20 or more pounds heavier than females, and one to two inches taller. That may not seem like a lot, but you will notice the difference in your house in terms of "how much dog" it feels like you are living with.

Aesthetically, many first-time owners are drawn to males because they look so powerful and impressive. Their larger heads and masculine stature are hard to ignore.

It helps to think about Ridgeback gender differences in terms of our own sex-based stereotypes, as politically incorrect as that might be. Male Ridgebacks are very straightforward, uncomplicated and sweet. They are particularly endeared to females of any species, and will reserve a special affection and deference for them. In human terms, the prototypical male Ridgeback sits back on the couch, beer in hand, a hail-fellow-well-met type who is inclined to smile benignly but dodge your honey-do list.

Female Ridgebacks, by contrast, are more complicated. They are thinkers and planners. In a household with a male Ridgeback, they rule the roost, always out in front, setting the agenda and making plans for the future.

Many Ridgeback households have one of each. Most male Ridgebacks will defer to females of any breed, and intersex conflicts are rare. (Same-sex conflicts are not common, either: Many Ridgeback owners maintain households of multiple females and/or males with no incident.) Many male Ridgebacks I know seem relieved to have a female in charge, a sort of "Phew, glad she's handling that" attitude.

If you do decide to have two or more Ridgebacks, just be sure not to acquire two littermates or puppies near the same age at once. Ridgebacks need time to bond to you individually, and there is a real risk that littermates will bond to each other instead of you. As a result, not many breeders will sell more than one puppy from a litter to the same owner, unless there are extenuating circumstances.

Black vs. Brown (or "Liver") Nose

I won't send your head spinning with a dissertation on Ridgeback color genetics. Suffice

A brown-nose Ridgeback (above) has blue or green eyes at eight weeks; they eventually change to amber. A black-nose puppy (right) will have a much darker brown eye.

Photos: Jens Ratsey-Woodroffe

it to say that Ridgebacks come in two nose colors, black and brown, and both are equally correct according to the standard.

Because the black nose is dominant to brown, there are simply more of them. Many Ridgeback buyers prefer the black noses, though they often can't articulate why. Often, it has to do with pigment: Brown-nose Ridgebacks do not have black pigment, so they cannot have a dark eye, which gives a certain quality to the expression. The lighter amber eye of the liver nose, while correct according to the standard, can appear a little more piercing and intense.

That said, many Ridgeback breeders and a growing number of buyers are drawn to brown noses. While Ridgeback breeders rarely breed for color (more on that later), some have a preference for brown noses, or would like to own one some time in their breeding career.

Brown-nose fans sometimes assert that their dogs have a different temperament than their

black-nosed counterparts. They describe them as more energetic, more clownish and, well, just smarter. The jury is out, but what is clear is that this nose color does have its loyal fan base, just as the more numerically popular black noses do.

Black Mask vs. "Clean" Face

The term "mask" refers to the darker black color that appears on a dog's muzzle (or, in the case of a liver nose, the shade will be a dark brown, though it is often not as noticeable). This isn't a "mask" in the true sense of the word, as it is confined to the muzzle area and should not creep up above the eyes. That gives the appearance of a Great Dane or Mastiff, and is not desirable in a Ridgeback.

**Above: Brown nose with mask.
Below: Black nose with mask.
Bottom: Clean face.**

Photos: Theresa M. Lyons (top and middle) and Sally Fineburg (bottom)

Many prospective Ridgeback owners request a "black masked" dog, which is not too difficult for a breeder to accommodate: Because it is a dominant trait, many Ridgebacks do have masks. In fact, it can be difficult to find a "clean faced" dog that does not have this coloration on the muzzle.

Shades of Wheaten and "Off Colors"

Ridgebacks are all one color or, more correctly, one pattern of color, called "wheaten." Just like it sounds, "wheaten" is, quite simply, the color of wheat, which isn't so simple at all: Depending on its maturity, wheat can range from a pale, flaxen color to a deep, rich red just before it is harvested. If you look closely, you'll see that the wheaten hairs of a Ridgeback are banded, containing more than one shade of golden red. That is what gives the Ridgeback coat its vibrancy and warmth.

Most American Ridgeback breeders do not consider what shade of wheaten a dog is when planning breedings. No one says, "I'm breeding to Dog A because he has such a beautiful red coat." A breeder might say, "Dog A has a clear coat, and I

At right, light wheaten, a shade that is becoming almost impossible to find outside of the United States, Scandinavia and the United Kingdom.

am hoping that he cleans up the smutty-looking black hairs in my girl's coat." But that has to do with the absence of black guard hairs in the coat, and nothing to do with the shade of wheaten.

Many puppy buyers like Ridgebacks that are the darker shade of wheaten, and it is fine to have a preference. (Breeders can predict the color the puppy will be by looking at the top of the head – that is the color the adult dog will turn out to be.) But the shade of wheaten is hardly a determining factor in selecting a dog for pet or show – it is the cherry on the sundae if you happen to get the shade you prefer.

In some parts of the world, a near fetish for deep-red Ridgebacks has led to an alarming trend of dogs that are almost a monotone red, the color of Irish Setters.

Much more uncommon are "off colors" such as blue or black and tan. Blue Ridgebacks have a grayish cast to them, like a Weimaraner, and are seen more often in Europe than in the U.S. Black-and-tan Ridgebacks have the coloration of a Doberman Pinscher – solid black body with tan points. Some contend that the colors were introduced into the Ridgeback gene pool via "oops" breedings with those aforementioned breeds, but regardless of their origin, they are not correct Ridgeback colors. Breeders may produce them and place them as pets, but these are not colors that they should be striving to replicate in order to sell them as a "rare" Ridgeback color pattern.

Deciding Who Goes Where

In this chapter, I've discussed some of the cosmetic considerations that buyers may want to take into account when choosing a Ridgeback puppy. I haven't even nicked the subject of what breeders are looking for in their keepers, as that's an entire book of its own. Suffice it to say that once a Ridgeback breeder identifies those puppies with good ridges, correct bites, kink-free tails and no excessive white, the real sorting begins.

During the last few weeks that the puppies are in their care, breeders begin to take exhaustive notice of their conformation, or how they are put together. They "stack," or pose, the puppies on a table to better see their structure. They analyze how they move at the trot. They observe their temperaments, and how they respond to different stimuli. They compare them to each other and to related dogs to see if they have something important to contribute to their breeding program.

Oftentimes, these final determinations about who goes where are made in the final week before the puppies go home. One well-regarded school of thought, popularized by judge, author and speaker Pat Hastings, holds that the perfect time to evaluate puppies is two or three days before or after they turn eight weeks old. It's at that time, Hastings contends, that the puppies will be miniature versions of what they will become in adulthood. Any earlier or later, and differing growth rates can mask that predictive picture.

All this means that a breeder might not be able to tell you exactly which puppy you will be going home with until just a few days before pick-up. For example, if you want a pet male

A black-and-tan Ridgeback. The pattern is not common in the breed. *Photo: Rick Singer*

and the breeder has four boys with more or less perfect ridges, then you will need to wait until she determines who are the best show prospects among them before she decides who can go as a pet.

Because the breeder is juggling all these variables, she needs to know your must-haves, as well as your preferences: "I must have a male, and I prefer a brown nose if I can have one." "Male or female doesn't matter to me, but I definitely want a dog with a black mask." "I want a female that I can do agility with, so a sound structure is really important to me."

The breeder is the best person to gauge the temperament of your new puppy. If you have smaller children, she will select a more laid-back, unflappable puppy as opposed to a more reactive one. If you indicate that you'd love to do lure coursing, she can identify the puppy with the strongest prey drive.

Remember that the more specifications you have, the harder it is for the breeder to find them in one package. If you don't want to budge on any of them, realize that it may take a litter or two for the breeder to produce exactly what you are looking for. But if they are important to you, they should be worth the wait.

Chances are good that you will be relying primarily on the breeder to select your puppy for you. But because you've selected your breeder wisely, all usually works out in the end.

"Buy a Show Dog, See the World"

That quote from famous Afghan Hound breeder Sunny Shay meant that showing dogs exposes you to people, places and situations you might otherwise have never encountered.

These days, many people are simply too busy get deeply involved in the sport of dogs. But that doesn't mean that you should dismiss a breeder's request to consider a "show puppy."

• *Show dogs are not always "on the road."* Many breeders just simply want their dogs to be shown to their championship – something that is accomplished in a finite period of time. After that, many of these dogs become champions of the couch.

• *Showing dogs doesn't have to break the bank.* Yes, hiring a professional handler at $90 a show adds up. But many breeders are happy to handle any dog they bred for free. Often, the only cost the owner incurs are show entries, which can range from $20 to $30 per day, and perhaps the cost of the occasional handling class. But handling classes are invaluable for any Ridgeback, whether or not she ever sees the inside of a show ring: Exposure at an early age to different breeds of all sizes, colors and shapes will make your dog a well-adjusted canine citizen.

Photo: Theresa M. Lyons

• *Intact males and females are not impossible to manage.* Intact males will not be lifting their leg all over the house or dry-humping your living-room settee. So long as they are not living with a female in heat, they are relatively low-key, unremarkable housemates.

The only problem with managing an intact male is dog parks. Inevitably, there will be a problem with the neutered males at the park, who will object to your dog's unaltered status, and scuffles ensue. And, particularly in "progressive" urban centers, the sight of an intact male can rile up human passersby, who often will lecture you relentlessly about the evils of animal overpopulation.

As for females, the only time anyone will know yours is intact is when she comes into heat. Unlike humans, this does not happen monthly, though a surprising number of people think it does! Most Ridgeback females come into heat every eight to 12 months, for a period of three weeks. When a female is in heat, you'll need to keep her especially secure – never left unattended in the yard, for example – so she does not attract unwanted Romeos. "Britches" are available to ensure that the relatively small amount of discharge does not stain carpets or furniture.

Owning a show dog may not be your cup of tea. But at least know the ins and outs before dismissing it entirely.

Size Does Matter

"How big will my Ridgeback get?" It's a valid question, and one that new owners are often intensely curious about.

If your breeder has a good idea of how her line matures and is knowledgeable about the sizes of the dogs in her pedigree, she might be able to give you a good guess about what your Ridgeback puppy will grow into. But it will be just that: a guess. Size can be difficult to predict in young puppies, no matter how big their feet look: The scrawniest runt can grow into a giant, and a honker can inexplicably fizzle out.

In Ridgebacks, the tendency is often "the bigger, the better." But it's important to remember what all the Ridgeback standards across the globe say: A male Ridgeback should stand between 25 and 27 inches at the shoulder, or withers. Take a wooden yardstick, hold it perpendicular to the floor, and look at where 27 inches – lies. Chances are you'll be surprised at how relatively small that is. Then remember that this is the top of the Ridgeback standard – the very tallest that a Ridgeback male should be.

Ridgeback females should be correspondingly moderately sized: 24 and 26 inches tall at the withers, according to the standard.

The stereotypical Ridgeback puppy buyer is usually looking for "a big one." In truth, an 80- or 90-pound Ridgeback – which is about what a 27-inch male weighs – is more than enough dog for anyone. A dog larger than this not only would likely have more difficulty doing the job he was bred to do – cornering and pivoting and exhibiting great athleticism – but you'll feel the reverberations of that excess poundage in the house. The difference between a 27-inch, 90-pound Ridgeback and a 30-inch, 110-pound Ridgeback is significant, just as there is a significant difference between males and females in terms of size.

When someone boasts that their Ridgeback weighs 120 pounds, a knowledgeable fancier's first reaction is either "That dog is obese," or "He's big enough to be a pony." Neither is a good scenario.

If size is important to you, seek out a line that consistently produces it to maximize your chances of getting it, but remember that intentionally breeding Ridgebacks that are much larger than what the standard describes erodes the breed's all-important athleticism.

Ridgebacks and Other Dogs

The Ridgeback was developed as a pack hound – bred to work with other four-leggers to hunt and do whatever tasks his master required. Generally speaking, the modern Ridgeback retains this gregariousness with his own kind, though there are exceptions that prove the rule.

The best companion for a Ridgeback is another Ridgeback – or another dog of a suitable and complementary breed. Some breeds are too "serious" for life with Ridgebacks: Mastiffs or Akitas might find the Ridgeback's prey drive and clownishness to be irritating. Others are simply too frail or slight to withstand a Ridgeback's rather rough play style: Greyhounds, for example, might be too "crunchy" for life with an exuberant Ridgeback.

A male-female combination is ideal: The male Ridgeback will almost always defer to his female counterparts, and skirmishes will be rare if not nonexistent. There are some breeds in which having two dogs of the same sex in the same household is a very bad idea, but generally speaking this is not the case with Ridgebacks. Many breeders maintain multi-male households, or keep three or more females together without so much as a raised lip or wayward glance. For the average Ridgeback pet owner, keeping two males or two females should not be a problem, though there are individual cases where two dogs simply may not get along.

Often, there's nothing better to give an elderly dog an infusion of vitality than to bring a puppy into the household. Just be aware that even with a middle-aged dog, there will be a period of adjustment. Established adult Ridgebacks may need several weeks to months before they grudgingly accept the new puppy. Be sure to give the older dog space, and for the very elderly, be aware that the puppy's high-energy hijinks might be too much for your oldster. Ridgeback puppies are pretty intuitive, and after a few rebukes will soon get the message that grumpy grandpa is not a play candidate.

I want to reiterate: "Twins" are a very bad idea. Sometimes puppy buyers will decide that they want to buy littermates: They figure that they'll wind up with two Ridgebacks eventually, so why not do all the work in one shot? This is a supremely bad idea. Ridgeback puppies need individual attention and time in order to be well-adjusted canine citizens. If you keep littermates of the same age, they will very likely bond to each other instead of you. What you need in the first year of your puppy's life is an uninterrupted opportunity to create a relationship with your dog. It's difficult enough to maintain a Ridgeback puppy's focus without having a littermate around to distract her further.

Wait until your Ridgeback puppy has reached the year mark before adding another to the family.

Registered Names

When you get your new puppy from your breeder, the puppy should come with registration papers. In order to register your puppy, you must decide on a registered name. This is different from his "call name," or the name you call him every day.

Many breeders will require that your dog's registered name begin with their kennel name. For example, my contracts require that all puppies I have bred, regardless of whether they are show dogs or family pets, be registered with my kennel name, Revodana, as the first word of that registered name. Some breeders like to have themed litters – for example, they will ask that the name refer to a Beatles song, or something having to do with the color blue. Holiday litters invariably have Christmas themes.

This Ridgeback and Dalmatian are about evenly matched, and that shouldn't be surprising: The Ridgeback standard of the 1920s was based on that of the Dalmatian. But for the Ridgeback's wheaten color, slightly larger size and hallmark ridge, the two share a similar "blueprint." *Photo: Dreamstime*

The registered name can be related to the call name – for example, a dog named Turbo may have a racing- or speed-related registered name – but it's not a requirement.

It's smart to confirm with your breeder before finalizing the registered name. Perhaps another dog already has that name. Or maybe you are inadvertently using a phrase that might be misconstrued. Finally, there's a degree of decorum typically associated with registered names. They can be trendy and humorous and even a little risqué, but do you really wants to be the person who registered your dog as Hey Hoser Bring Me a Beer?

And there really was a Ridgeback with that name.

Chapter 5

Welcome Home: Crating, Housetraining, Inhibition and Leash Walking

When it comes to polite house manners, the good news is that Ridgebacks are relatively quick learners. You just need consistency, the right tools and a cohesive plan.

Please don't underestimate that first ingredient: Ridgebacks are very intelligent, and if you are as clear and consistent as possible, they will quickly catch on. Though they are stubborn at times, they do want to learn, and can be very pleased with themselves when they've done something right, and you tell them as much. So, heavy on the praise, and ease up on the negativity. You'll get there a lot faster if you do.

Crate Training

As recently as 20 years ago, crates were a relative novelty. Today, they are considered as basic a piece of equipment as a collar or leash.

Every Ridgeback puppy needs a crate. It is not a cage, but rather a retreat – the one place where your puppy can go to have his own space. If there are any children in your household, make it abundantly clear that they are not permitted in the crate; it has to be a place that they respect as the dog's sanctuary – no exceptions. Children, especially preschoolers, think a crate is the coolest kind of playhouse – it's small, it's snug, it's forbidden, and therefore irresistible. When my children were small, I reserve the sternest rebuke for any kind of messing around with the dogs' crates – not only going in them, but opening them without permission.

There are many types and styles of crates; each one works best in slightly different situations.

Plastic crates are also called airline crates, and a popular brand is the Vari Kennel. If your dog ever has to be transported in an airplane, it's imperative that he be comfortable in this type of crate. Most plastic crates are two pieces of molded plastic – top and bottom – that attach in the middle with specially made screws. This makes them easy to store when not in use: Just separate the two halves and nest them inside one another.

I prefer to use a plastic crate for the first two to six months of a puppy's life, for reasons I'll explain in a second; then I switch to a wire crate.

Since many male Ridgebacks average about 27 inches in height, give or take an inch in either direction, you might want to get an extra large; most females are comfortable in a large.

e visibility for the puppy to see what's going on in the
them is that rambunctious young puppies can get their
I only use a metal crate when I am around to supervise
r so, the puppy will have grown enough so that this jaw-
ern.

ove your puppy's collar when crating him in a metal
an strangle himself if the tags get caught between the

de out of nylon. These lightweight crates are good for
those times when you will be in eyeshot of your crated Ridgeback (such as at a family
party). Never leave a Ridgeback unsupervised in a mesh crate; he'll soon learn to roll it,
like one of those hamsters inside a plastic ball, or chew through it.

Crate Tips

*No matter what type of crate you choose, buy the size that your dog will fit into as an
adult.* A crated puppy should only have enough room to turn around in – any roomier,
and the puppy will cheerfully start eliminating in the crate. You can take a cardboard
box and put it at the back of the crate to take up the excess room. As your puppy grows,
replace the box with a correspondingly smaller one.

how long can the dog stay in the crate?

Like any tool, a crate can be misused: Do not leave a puppy in a crate for more than four
hours at a stretch. If you work full time and there is no one home during the day, you'll
need to hire a pet sitter to come by at least twice a day during the first few weeks to let the
puppy out, feed and water her, and let her romp around. As your puppy gets older, you
can decrease the visits to once a day, presuming you will be gone for a typical eight-hour
day. Remember that even though you have arrived home from a long, tiring day, your
puppy will be raring to go after a day of confinement. Plan on a long walk, puppy playdate,
training class or other strenuous physical or mental exercise to burn off that energy.

Foster a positive association with the crate by feeding your puppy in it. Keep the door
open so he can come and go at will. Leave surprise caches of food or treats in the crate, so
he makes a habit of popping in regularly to see if any goodies have materialized. (You can
do the same in the bathtub – no water, of course – to help make that an enticing place, too,
once he gets big enough to hop in. That advance conditioning will make winter bathtime
sessions much easier.)

*The age at which a dog can be trusted to be left loose in the house when you leave
depends entirely on the individual dog.* Some Ridgebacks can be trusted to be left alone
loose by a year of age; some need to reach age two before they leave pillow pillaging and
couch destuffing behind. Start slowly, with five, then 10 minutes alone; gradually lengthen
the time you leave the dog.

Never let a puppy out of her crate if she is barking. If you do, you teach your Ridgeback a

56

Fabric crates like this one, which often have zip tops, are fine for temporary crating when you are nearby, but most Ridgebacks will escape from them if left unattended for too long. *Photo: Dreamstime*

very dangerous lesson: Barking is what gains me my freedom. The longer she barks before you give in and open the door, the worse it becomes: You've just taught her to bark longer and longer to get what she wants. Make sure your puppy is quiet – even if it's just for a few seconds – before you open that crate door. If you think of it, attach a word to the behavior you want: Say, "Quiet, good quiet," when she has stopped vocalizing as you open the door.

A tired puppy is a good puppy. Regular exercise – both mental and physical – will leave your puppy less inclined to be destructive. Err on the side of too little time when leaving your puppy alone; start with a short period, and increase with smaller increments.

Housetraining

Some breeds are better than others with housebreaking, and with a Ridgeback, you are in luck: Provided you are vigilant and consistent, and use a lot of positive reinforcement, your puppy will soon learn that it is inappropriate to relieve himself in the house.

A puppy has one hour of bowel/bladder control for every month of her life. So a 2-month-old puppy, which is how old your Ridgeback will be when you take her home, needs to relieve herself every two hours or so.

Find out what your puppy will be eliminating on in the whelping box, and see if you can use some in your outside area to help with transitioning. Many breeders designate *what is this?*

a portion of their whelping area as a "potty," and use various substrates underfoot, such as shredded newspaper (which is becoming surprisingly rare in our digital world!) or wood shavings. I prefer biodegradable, chemical-free compressed wood pellets, which are used as fuel for wooden stoves or as horse bedding and are sold at most feed stores; they simply disintegrate into sawdust when wet, and can be easily scooped up. (I buy mine at Agway for $8 for a 40-pound bag.) For puppy owners who have backyards where they want their puppies to eliminate, I provide a small bag filled with the pellets to act as a transition while the puppy learns to eliminate outside. *put some outside*

A devastating scene – and guilty party – that will be familiar to many Ridgeback owners. *Photo: Daren Hom*

Avoid mistakes before they happen by anticipating when your puppy is most likely to urinate or defecate. Key times are after eating, drinking, playing or sleeping. While it may seem subtle, a puppy who is sniffing and moving around quickly is likely signaling her intent to produce an "oops" in the next couple of seconds. Take her outside, and praise her lavishly when she potties there. (Better yet, give her a treat.)

Occasionally, puppy buyers will ask about using "wee-wee" pads, especially if they live in an apartment building and can't always hustle the puppy outside in enough time to avoid an accident. I usually suggest they use the same wood pellets that I do: I have had many owners in Manhattan get through tough New York winters with a new puppy by training him to use a shallow tray of pellets in their bathroom or kitchen.

Your greatest downfall in the housetraining department will be inconsistency. In the house, do not allow your unhousebroken Ridgeback out of your view for a second; every "mistake" you do not catch will only confuse the puppy more. The ideal is to never allow the puppy to urinate or defecate without being caught, scooped up and shown the appropriate place where he is expected to relieve himself.

If you have area rugs, temporarily cover them with cheap plastic sheeting, the kind painters use, available at any hardware store. (The heavier the mil, the better.) This will save your rugs, and prevent your Ridgeback from returning to the scene of previous mistakes. It will also give you an auditory cue ... when you hear that pitter-patter on plastic, get over there quick!

Crating your puppy in your bedroom at night is ideal; your puppy will wake up and whimper when he has to go outside. Some puppies are very compliant and sleep until morning from day one. But expect to be getting up at 3 a.m. until your puppy's bladder matures and he can sleep through the night. Ah, the joys of parenthood!

Did I mention Ridgebacks hate rain? And snow? Well, they do, often with a passion. Even many house-trained adult Ridgebacks will look at you pathetically and refuse to do their business outside when it's too cold or wet. In those cases, I treat the adult just as I would the puppy: Inside, back in the crate, then try again 10 minutes later. Eventually, out of sheer boredom or the shrill call of nature, they do relieve themselves. Make sure you are there to praise them and let them back in when they do, so they associate that action with what they want, which is to get inside where it is warm and dry. I have had Ridgebacks that have faked eliminating – they squat, even though they don't urinate – just to convince me to let them back in. Smart dogs!

Most Ridgebacks enjoy a frolic in the snow (above), but they'd really prefer to be warm and toasty (below).

Baby, It's Cold Outside!

Ridgebacks come from southern Africa, a part of the world that's not exactly known for its frigid temperatures. Despite the fact that they generally prefer heat to cold, today Ridgebacks live all over the globe, including places as frosty as Russia and Alaska. Being sturdy and stoic dogs, Ridgebacks can certainly tolerate some time out in the snow or freezing weather, especially if they're involved in activity and are moving around. But sustained exposure to freezing temperatures – especially living outdoors in the elements – is entirely unsuitable for a Ridgeback.

When it comes to taking your Ridgeback out in cold weather, let the dog be your guide. If he is walking or running briskly, with not a lot of opportunity to stand around and get chilled, oftentimes he'll do just fine. But if the time outside is prolonged, or your dog is doing a lot of standing around, a winter coat is a good idea. Remember, too, that the chemicals used to prevent icing on wintry streets and sidewalks can be harsh and caustic on your dog's pads. If you or your neighbors use those kinds of products, consider investing in a pair of snow booties.

Bite Inhibition

One of the biggest complaints that breeders get from new puppy owners is that their new family member is doing an excellent impersonation of an alligator.

This isn't a cause for concern: Dogs naturally communicate with their mouths, and Ridgebacks are very "chatty." Your job from the minute your new puppy arrives home is to teach her that nipping is unacceptable; you are not a chew toy; and if she does use her mouth, she needs to learn the appropriate level of pressure to apply – in other words, she has to have a "soft mouth."

Don't just tell your Ridgeback "no"; give her a "yes" to chew on instead. In other words, when your puppy decides to start gnawing on your wrist, give her an appropriate toy to chew on instead and praise her for chewing it.

(no + yes to chew + praise)

Appropriate chew toys include Kongs stuffed with peanut butter or cheese and then frozen (the company makes mini-sized Kongs that are perfect for 8-week-old Ridgeback puppies); Nylabones; wet washcloths that are wrung and then frozen (these are especially soothing when the puppy is teething).

Feeling like a chew toy yourself? That's a major concern I get from new owners whose puppies are simply gnawing on them like there's no tomorrow; even worse are the drive-by nippings.

One way to deal with this is to let out a very sharp yelp, almost like a puppy that's been bitten too hard by a littermate. In theory, you are communicating to the puppy in "her" language that her play style is too forceful. This works with some puppies; others are oblivious, and may even bite at you harder in their excitement.

A better solution is to simply stop interacting with the puppy when she gets too "mouthy." Say "Ouch" or "Too bad" or whatever code word you want to use to signal that her behavior has just crossed a line, and then make yourself physically unavailable, so she

Above, puppies learn bite inhibition from playing with littermates. *Photo: Jens Ratsey-Woodroffe*
Below, "seek higher ground" in action.

can no longer interact with you. Put her in a crate, or behind a baby gate, if only for a minute or two, then try again. If she again starts biting too hard, repeat the process.

This sounds like a lot of work, and it is, but Ridgeback puppies are smart puppies, and if you are consistent it won't be long before yours figures out that the only way to be with you is to behave.

Teach the command "Seek higher ground" – to your children, that is. Young children, and even older ones, can become frustrated and even upset with a teething Ridgeback puppy. Oftentimes, they will express this by shrieking and running away from the puppy, which only encourages the behavior they don't want.

When my children were small, I taught them "Seek higher ground," which meant that they ought to go somewhere where the Ridgeback puppy cannot reach them. Originally, I intended this for food, to avoid those drive-by peanut-butter-and-jelly incidents that are so common when you mix Ridgeback puppies with young humans, but it works for nipping and teething, too. The puppy soon learns that if he is too rough, his human playmate will not want to interact with him anymore.

This young Ridgeback is wearing a martingdale-style collar. No matter how she might pull, she cannot wriggle out of it. *Photo: Suzanne Humenik*

A word about rawhide: Some owners dislike giving their dogs rawhide because it is not digestible, and they are concerned that the dog might swallow a small piece. I always remove rawhide once it gets to that size, and have never had a problem. However, I am very careful to only buy rawhide that has been made and processed in the United States. Rawhide from Mexico and Central and South America can be treated with formaldehyde. Be sure to read labels carefully: Rawhide that is "made from American cows" can still be processed outside of the U.S. – and often is.

What about marrow bones and deer antlers? As someone who feeds a raw diet (more about that later), I have no problem giving dogs biologically appropriate objects to chew on; in recent years, naturally shed deer antlers have become a popular chew treat, especially for large breeds such as Ridgebacks. Be aware, however, that dogs can and do crack their adult teeth on bones and antlers. And I can tell you from experience that if you have taxidermy in the house, encouraging Ridgebacks to chew on those calcium-rich antlers may lead them to prospect on what is hanging from the walls for a late-night snack!

Leash Walking

When out and about with his family and friends, a Ridgeback's natural inclination is to travel slightly ahead, in order to anticipate what is coming. It is a normal instinct, but one that can soon morph into industrial-strength pulling when on leash.

Start leash training as soon as your puppy arrives home.

Get a martingale collar. For a general-purpose, all-round collar, I prefer a martingale. These collars are made of flat nylon, like a regular buckle collar, but have two loops: The large loop goes around the dog's neck; the small loop goes through either end of the large loop, and the leash attaches to it. When the dog pulls, the small loop tightens the larger one, making it very difficult for the dog to back out of the collar.

Remember to remove collars during playtime. Though it does not happen often, dogs can hook their jaws on the collar of a playmate and get stuck there. In the ensuing panic, dogs can be severely injured and even break their necks or jaws.

Make leash walking fun. The first time your puppy goes for a walk on leash with you, he may balk and refuse to go forward. This is your first opportunity to use positive reinforcement to get your Ridgeback to do what you want. Entice him to move forward with treats. If you are using clicker training (see Chapter 7), click for the slightest slackness in the collar, or for the puppy coming along in the direction you want.

No leash chewing. Ridgeback puppies love to gnaw on leashes as they are walking, or if you stop for any reason and they are bored. Be aware of this and stop it immediately. It takes only a couple of minutes for a busy Ridgeback to nibble through an expensive leather or nylon leash.

Be a tree. Once your puppy gets accustomed to the leash, you will have the opposite problem: He will start to pull.

Basically, any time your Ridgeback pulls, you stop. Plant your roots – hence the "Be a tree" – and refuse to move until he gives you some slack in the leash and comes back to you. At first, this will be time consuming, and you won't get very far, but if you stick with it, your puppy will soon learn that in order to get what he wants – to move forward and explore –

A head halter might look like a muzzle, but it isn't; the mouth is not impeded. What the halter does do is control the head so the dog can't pull or lunge. *Photo: ThruMarzenasLens.com*

he needs to keep some slack on the leash.

Trust me: There is nothing more annoying than a Ridgeback who is yanking your arm off every second of a walk.

The cure for unrepentant pullers is a head halter. If you do not succeed at teaching your Ridgeback to be a polite non-puller on the leash, a head halter will stop him in his tracks. Made of nylon and modeled on the halters worn by horses, these are sometimes mistaken for muzzles, but they are not.

The head halter operates under the principle of "Control the head, and you control the dog." The head halter loops around the muzzle, and the leash attaches under the jaw. This makes the dog unable to forge ahead.

There are several important caveats with the head halter: First, the dog needs to be introduced to it slowly; you can't just slap it on and be on your way. Plan on several sessions with treats so he can get used to the sensation of the halter, particularly across his nose; most Ridgebacks will try to paw at it, or rub their faces against furniture or your leg to try to get rid of it.

Second, be aware that you can inflict severe damage to the dog's neck if you jerk the head halter. Slow, steady pressure on the halter is all that is needed to control the dog.

Please don't use a prong collar. There's nothing that makes a Ridgeback lover wince more than the sight of one of those medieval torture devices around the neck of one of our beautiful hounds. For a very bad puller, the head halter described above is much more humane, not to mention more effective.

Please Remember

All the situations described in this chapter – crate training, housebreaking, leash walking and bite inhibition – are temporary. When your Ridgeback puppy joins your household, there are going to be adjustments, and mistakes, and, yes, messes. When you are in the midst of them, they can seem overwhelming. Just remember that your Ridgeback puppy will soon – maybe even altogether too soon – grow into a more predictable, calm adult. Your dog will not be a needle-toothed alligator for the rest of his life. He will eventually get the concept of peeing outside the house and not inside it. His biggest factor for success is *you*: If you are thoughtful and patient, if you identify problems early on and then find reasonable solutions, then these little homecoming hiccups will pass quickly … Until, that is, you decide to get that *next* Ridgeback puppy to keep your now perfectly behaved, grown-up one company.

Chapter 6

Temperament and Socialization

Several years ago, a Ridgebacker posted to a popular email list expressing concern at the temperaments she had seen at a dog show that weekend: Dogs that growled. Dogs that shied away from the judge and refused to be examined. Dogs that bucked like broncos and pulled their handlers to the exit.

I've seen those displays plenty of times before. But oftentimes, it's not the dogs – or their breeding – that is to blame. Instead, it's the other end of the lead that deserves the scrutiny.

With his incredible athleticism and imposing presence, a Ridgeback looks like a tough guy who can handle whatever the world can dish out. In part, this is true: The Ridgeback has great courage and stamina. But he is a thinking dog, a hound with a sensitive, soft nature beneath that brave exterior. One would not expect an Afghan Hound to respond gleefully to a collar pop. Why should a Ridgeback be any different?

Heavy-handed tactics have little success on Ridgebacks, yet it is not uncommon to see some owners trying to "train" their dogs by jerking their leads and popping them under the jaw. Forceful handling that a Sporting or Herding dog might take in stride can send a Ridgeback into a tailspin, especially if it is administered by someone whom the dog does not know or, more importantly, trust.

As with most things, breed history speaks volumes on this subject. Ridgebacks were bred to hunt large and dangerous game, relying on their own intelligence and judgment. These dogs are not hard-wired to consult their owners; in the field, that kind of distraction meant the difference between life and death. So with the Ridgeback, as with most hounds and terriers, human omniscience is not a given.

As a result, if a Ridgeback is confronted with a new experience with which he is not comfortable, he will not reflexively cede to the will of his handler. I once saw this point delivered wordlessly but most elegantly by a Ridgeback who not only reared up and bolted from her handler in the show ring, but gave him a shiner in the process.

Does this mean that a Ridgeback cannot be made to mind his owner? Of course not. But it does mean that the intelligence of the breed must be respected. If you have a true understanding of this breed, you know how to build trust and how to negotiate with the dog to arrive at the same place together, both literally and figuratively. This may go a long way toward explaining why Ridgebacks seem to show so much more willingly for female handlers, who, at the risk of indulging in gender stereotypes, can be more flexible and intuitive.

Within every breed, there are ranges in temperament, and this is of course true for the Ridgeback. Some dogs are more laidback than others. Some are more reactive. Some

have stronger prey drives. Some are more attuned to their owners, and as a result more biddable. But they should all share this mix of intelligence and sensitivity that is part of their "Ridgebackness."

Evolution of Ridgeback Temperament

In every breed, temperaments continually develop and fine-tune, based on the society in which the dog lives: In some parts of the world, there's an emphasis on guarding function, while elsewhere the dog may be required to have more of a hunting role.

This has been the case with the Ridgeback long before its inception as a formal breed. In some parts of southern Africa, the Ridgeback was required to be more of a protector. In other parts, he was primarily a hunter. The two roles require different temperaments, and for that matter, oftentimes different physiques. This is why – along with the relative newness of the breed, and the infusion of many foundation breeds – we see such diversity Ridgebacks, from stouter,

Ridgeback temperaments have come a long way, baby. *Photo: Allison Clancy*

cobbier, "bullier" types to rangier, lighter-boned, more "Sighthound"-looking examples. (The ideal dog, of course, is in the middle.)

The early Ridgebacks that were imported into the United States in the 1950s and well into the 1960s had relatively edgy temperaments. They were frequently described as "one-man dogs," and aggression toward people was not unheard of. In a word, these were tough dogs. And owners needed a firm hand to keep them in line.

In short order, American breeders soon softened these flinty temperaments. Careful selection of dogs with stable characters – who were, as the breed standard requires, diffident toward strangers but not hostile – soon became the norm. Today, ironically, the breed has arguably gone too much in this direction, with happy-go-lucky, goofy temperaments that seem more apt for a Labradoodle than a hunting hound like the Ridgeback.

Stranger Danger

The Ridgeback standard calls for a dog that is "reserved with strangers." "Reserved" means that your Ridgeback will consider and treat a stranger just as humans do their own kind: He will be polite, perhaps offer a formal greeting, then go about his business. If the stranger has something of interest – whether a piece of cheese or a novel scent on his trouser leg – the Ridgeback might dally a bit more.

But the Ridgeback understands that there are strangers, and there are friends, and even among friends there are gradations of intimacy. In this way, he is no different from you or me. He does not treat everyone with the same exuberance. If you have a history with him, if he has grown to love you, you will be greeted more effusively than someone he's known for only five minutes. It's this discretion and intelligence that we so value in the breed. That's not to say that a stranger is met with hostility: again, indifference is the word.

Play Style

Ridgebacks are athletic and physical dogs – they love to use their bodies when they play. If you watch a Ridgeback interacting with a group of "average dogs," you'll see this difference immediately. The Ridgeback zips around, body-slams, pivots, turns, leaps – it's a ballet of explosive energy. Obviously this play style is not always compatible with every breed of dog, for reasons both physical and temperamental. There are just some breeds that physically can't withstand being body-slammed by a Ridgeback at 25 miles per hour. This isn't just small breeds like Toy dogs, but also larger but finer-boned ones such as Greyhounds.

Conversely, there are some very sturdy breeds – such as Akitas and Bullmastiffs – that could easily withstand a Ridgeback's playful onslaughts, but who find that kind of energy to be over the top and disrespectful. Encounters with these more "serious" breeds will not end well.

If you understand Ridgeback play style, you know that acrobatic displays such as these are usually just all in good fun. *Photo: Dreamstime*

The best playmate for a Ridgeback – other than another Ridgeback, of course – is a breed that has a good nature and a relatively solid physique. Labrador and Golden retrievers

Ridgebacks generally do not love water, but there are exceptions.
Photo: Karin Van Klaveren | Dreamstime

are often sturdy enough to play with Ridgebacks. Boxers and Pitbulls have the same acrobatic, body-slamming style, and so as long as they're temperamentally inclined, they can make great Ridgeback playmates. Keep in mind that a dog that is an appropriate match for your Ridgeback puppy at four months old might not be so appropriate once your Ridgeback reaches full height and weight.

In the end, the proof is in the pudding. Intensely supervised encounters with a potential playmate will let you know whether or not these two are suitable for each other.

Ridgebacks typically play hard. To the uninitiated, it might even look like they are "disagreeing," but most of the time nothing could be further from the truth.
Photo: Dreamstime

Dogs of any breed have natural, not aggressive behaviors that can be misinterpreted by those who don't understand canine body language. Two growling, nipping, biting puppies could very well be playing appropriately – or they could be escalating to a not-so-pleasant conclusion. The way to know the difference is to become attuned to canine body language.

Ridgebacks and Water

As a general rule, Ridgebacks are not enthusiastic water dogs. They could take it or leave it – and most are very happy to leave it. This indifference makes sense when you consider the land of their origins. In Africa, a small mammal like your Ridgeback in a pool of standing water is an inviting target for lunch. This may go a long way to explain the Ridgeback's dislike for jumping into any standing body of water. Instead, the dogs prefer to wade into a graded entry point. In that way, perhaps they think they can assess the possibility of any predator lying in wait.

That's not to say that it's impossible to get Ridgebacks to swim, but, as with anything else that they are not naturally inclined to do, it will take a bit of effort. Be sure that any and all encounters with water are intensely positive. The Ridgeback that was flung into the swimming pool in the spirit of "sink or swim" will probably keep a wide berth forevermore.

Ridgebacks often will trot around proudly with a "prize" in their mouth. But ask them to fetch for you, and it's an entirely different story. *Photo: Pat Hoffmann*

Fetching

This will be a short section, because Ridgebacks don't fetch. You can throw a ball, and your Ridgeback might chase it, but chances are, once it stops moving, he will, too. The drive to bring the ball and drop it adoringly at your feet simply isn't there. The Ridgeback's reaction is more akin to, "Well, if you threw it away, why would you ever want it back?"

Territoriality

Ridgebacks are not particularly territorial dogs – that is, they aren't as hard-wired as some true guarding breeds to stake their piece of land and defend it at all costs. In a very general sense, Ridgebacks are more focused on people rather than property. That's not to say that a Ridgeback will stand idly by if someone breaks into your home in the dead of night. But that Ridgeback won't be thinking about the homestead, per se. He'll be thinking about *you*.

Lure-coursing is a great way to channel your Ridgeback's prey drive. *Photo: Jens Ratsey-Woodroffe*

Prey Drive

Ridgebacks chase things – simple as that. This instinct to pursue is hard-wired into the breed. It's what makes them so very good at lure coursing, a sort of simulated rabbit hunt in which the "prey" is a kitchen garbage bag tied to a continuous loop. Watching a Ridgeback zip around a football field in pursuit of a white slip of plastic tells you more eloquently than I could ever just how much these dogs love the thrill of the hunt.

Some Ridgebacks have little to no prey drive; they'd much prefer to stay glued to Mommy's side than run after anything. Still others possess a desire to please their humans that is so strong it can override the urge to chase whatever varmint is in view. But the vast majority of Ridgebacks are, simply, too prey driven to be reliable off leash.

So does this mean your Ridgeback can never run free? If you find a very remote or secure place – a secluded beach, a fenced schoolyard – you might conclude it is relatively safe to let your Ridgeback off leash. Program a strong "come" command by never using that word unless your dog is in a frame of mind to want to obey it, and always with a very delicious treat as a reward. Even then, some distractions might prove too strong for your Ridgeback – so get in the habit of spotting them before he does.

Traditional and Electric Fences

Being consummate athletes, Ridgebacks are more than capable of vaulting over even a six-foot fence. The key is never giving them the opportunity. Even if your property is fully and securely fenced, it's best not to leave your Ridgeback unsupervised for long periods of time, and certainly not if you are leaving the house.

Some owners have had success in getting their Ridgebacks to respect the "invisible" boundaries of an electric fence because the shock issued when crossing them can be very offputting to our sensitive hounds. But others note that the breed's souped-up prey drive can prompt a Ridgeback in hot in pursuit of a squirrel to blow right through the fence; by the time he realizes he has received a shock, he could very well be on the other side of the electrical current, and cannot re-enter without shocking himself again.

While electric fences might keep certain Ridgebacks *on* your property, they do nothing to keep intruders *off* it. Strange dogs are free to wander over, and your Ridgeback, restricted to the area by his shock collar, cannot retreat from any threat. Just as problematic, strangers and children can cross your property, leaving you open to liability if your Ridgeback were to knock them down.

If you must have an electric fence with your Ridgeback, be sure to use a reputable company that will introduce the fence properly, so your dog is not confused or unnecessarily zapped when learning its electronic boundaries. And never leave your dog unattended when it is in use; always be there to supervise.

Encourage friendships with a diverse assortment of well-behaved canines.

Give your Ridgeback the time and space to process new experiences.

How to Raise a Stable, Well-Adjusted Ridgeback

Temperament – the way a dog reacts with and to the world around him – is a product of nature and nurture. Breeders will argue about which has more currency, and my thoughts on that have evolved over the years. I used to believe that events in a puppy's upbringing could severely affect temperament, in particular negatively. These days, I am more inclined to think that this is the exception rather than the rule. Ridgebacks with stable temperaments are able to overcome negative experiences; one bad encounter will not "ruin them for life." By comparison, high-strung and reactive Ridgebacks can be unsettled and unglued by a seemingly benign, everyday occurrence.

This doesn't mean that you should expose your Ridgebacks to situations where he will feel vulnerable or frightened; of course, do your utmost to avoid them. But it does mean that on balance, lots of positive reinforcement and early and frequent socialization will help immeasurably in making your Ridgeback a stable, unflappable ambassador for the breed.

Don't miss the socialization "window." While curiosity and the ability to learn don't have expiration dates, young puppies have an important behavioral "sweet spot" between the ages of eight and 16 weeks. During this critical three-month period, your Ridgeback

74

builds her impressions and attitudes about what is normal and acceptable. More than any other, positive experiences with the world around her build a so... foundation for the rest of your dog's hopefully long life.

But in the buffet of sensory stimulation that your puppy encounters, make sure her experience is a quick snack rather than a binge. A visit to your child's soccer game, for instance, can do more harm than good if you are distracted, a pack of kids swarms the cute new puppy, and someone's snarky Schnoodle meanders over to chomp instead of chat. Less really can be more.

exposure to outside world

Finally, remember that socialization isn't just about exposure to new people and places. It's about acclimating your Ridgeback to all sorts of details: hairdryers, people who might have a physical tic or odd gait, skateboarders and cyclists, people wearing uniforms, manhole covers, lawn mowers, car rides, even bad weather. The list goes on and on.

Be a class act. Puppy kindergarten classes are a great way for puppies as young as eight weeks old to meet other dogs and people, provided it is in a controlled environment. A good class will require your Ridgeback to have had at least one set of vaccines, and will disinfect the classroom space before puppies assemble.

Before plunking down your cash and signing up, visit a session without your puppy. Watch and see how the instructors manage the class. Are they watching out for different breed-specific playing styles? Are they intervening and redirecting behavior that might escalate to something unpleasant?

Ridgebacks and cats can get along if the cat sets the ground rules early on.
Photos: Suzanne Humenik

should not be a no-holds-barred romper room. Even if they
man kindergarteners play, they are being taught important social
rol and respect for others, and it should be the same with their furry
he mosh pit.

this time

y pack. Because of their hunting history and the breeds that were used
to deve   idgebacks are extraordinarily visual. So if your Ridgeback grows up
only knowing Ridgebacks, he'll usually react with a waggy-tailed familiarity to Boxers and
Vizslas and Pitbulls, thinking them just mildly different versions of himself. But such a
Ridgeback's first encounter with a black Standard Poodle or a fluffy white Great Pyrenees
is very likely to have a different outcome.

To avoid this culture shock, young Ridgebacks need to interact with as many different
kinds of dogs as possible, as early as possible. Different sizes, shapes, coat textures, colors
and play styles – the more variety, the better. The only caveat is that all these dogs need
to be well mannered and friendly toward other dogs, and especially young puppies.
Otherwise you're inviting an even bigger problem.

First impressions count. They say you never have a second chance to make a first
impression, and that goes double for Ridgeback puppies. If a Ridgeback has a negative
experience, especially in puppyhood, he tends to generalize it. So if your carefree
Ridgeback puppy is accosted by an Alaskan Malamute at the dog run, chances are he will
carry that vendetta toward spitz-type dogs forward, perhaps for his entire lifetime.

Conversely, a positive association that's made early on can lead to a lifelong infatuation.
For example, as I said earlier, Ridgebacks do not typically like water. My first female
Ridgeback learned how to swim at the water's edge by gobbling hot-dog slices out of
the surf. (When cut into little medallion slices, hot dogs are very buoyant – ideal for
teaching a puppy how to swim.) This positive correlation between a favorite treat and
the wet stuff was so strong that any time she got a whiff of saltwater, she fairly exploded
with excitement. On land, she was as indifferent to a game of fetch as any red-blooded
Ridgeback. But in a body of water, she was a born-again Labrador Retriever, slapping the
water with her paws and barking her demand that you throw a stick or ball. It was all due
to that early imprinting.

Acknowledge fear periods. Ridgebacks periodically go through "fear periods," in which
they might be afraid of objects or situations that previously were not an issue. Your
normally outgoing and unflappable Ridgeback may all of a sudden be freaked out by
something as simple as opening an umbrella, or a newly hung painting on the wall. These
intensely emotional times usually correlate with developmental stages and growth spurts,
and typically happen between eight and 11 weeks, and then again at six and 14 months.

It's important to recognize these fear periods for what they are – periods that will
eventually be over. It's your job to nurture your Ridgeback puppy through them.

The best way to deal with fear periods is to be sensible. On the one hand, you don't want
to lock your dog up so he has no exposure to new things, even though they might have the

potential of frightening him. On the other hand, you don't want to immerse him so deeply in an upsetting experience that you make matters worse.

Take that scary umbrella. The first step is to overcome your dog's fear of the umbrella while it's closed. Put in the middle of the floor and surround it with delicious treats. Hopefully, your puppy eventually approaches, and starts snacking. Continue for a few more sessions, until he is comfortable, then bring the treats closer. When he's happily chomping away, next time place them on the umbrella itself. Next open the umbrella, and scatter the treats a reasonable distance away. If you keep progressing like this, incrementally, eventually you'll have your Ridgeback nibbling his treats from inside the open umbrella. From there, it's a short step to having him react to the opening of an umbrella with pleasant anticipation instead of fear.

Despite what the hype says, Ridgebacks were not bred to "take down" lions. Instead, they used their wits to outmaneuver the king of beasts. That intelligence and athleticism can sometimes be a challenge to unsuspecting new owners. *Photo: Denise Flaim*

Be firm. Like any independent breed, Ridgebacks need a leader. They don't do well with owners who are wishy-washy, who can't make up their own minds, who waiver at every fork in the road. Ridgebacks abhor a vacuum, and if they perceive that you are not in control, they will feel compelled to take the leadership role on for themselves. As you can imagine, that can lead to a dog becoming overly protective, reactive or territorial.

This isn't to say that if you're a quiet, contemplative, low-key person you shouldn't own a Ridgeback. There are plenty of outspoken and energetic people who would be

destabilizing for a Ridgeback. The bottom line is that, wh[...]
the Ridgeback has to believe that you know who you are [...]
going and you've got it under control. He needs to know [...]
unquestionably the primary decision-maker. He's in the p[...]

Be flexible. This duality is the most fascinating – and, argu[...]
the Ridgeback. On the one hand, you can't be too permissiv[...]
too demanding. Ridgebacks want strong leaders, but they d[...]
be open to a little give-and-take when you have a Ridgeback[...]
independent spirit, that he doesn't consider you omniscient, [...]
just that – a relationship. Using aversive, punishment-based t[...] as your
primary training tool will spell disaster with a Ridgeback. Compare it to raising a child:
Successful, well-adjusted children come from households where they are encouraged and
praised for what they do right; while their mistakes and misbehaviors are acknowledged,
they don't become the primary focus.

Treat your Ridgeback like a dog – not a child substitute. I don't agree with all of what
Cesar Millan preaches, but I do agree with this: Many of the behavior problems we see in
dogs are attributable to the fact that their owners treat them like little humans in fur suits
instead of the domesticated animals that they are.

A Ridgeback is not a baby. A Ridgeback is an independent, athletic, large dog that, if not
properly trained, can quickly turn into a liability.

Ridgeback puppies are exceptionally cute. They suck you in with their limpid eyes and
their floppy ears. The fact that they love their creature comforts, that they snuggle up to
you with big contented sighs in the evening, can lead you to think that they are charming,
angelic creatures. Once lulled into this sense of complacency you won't see adolescence
coming. You won't see the point where that cherubic Ridgeback puppy becomes an
intense, physically motivated, opinionated teenager.

Make some things non-negotiable. It is crucial that while your Ridgeback puppy is still
small and impressionable that you teach her that she must accept certain things that she
might otherwise not wish to. Nail cutting is at the top of this list. I can't tell you how many
Ridgebacks I know that the age of three and four months put up such a fuss about having
their nails clipped or Dremeled that their owner stopped doing it. Six months later, they
discover that their once-cute puppy's nails have grown into unmanageable talons that are
so long they are beginning to distorts the shape of her feet. And she is unwilling to tolerate
them even being touched, much less trimmed.

From the moment you get her, your puppy should learn that there are just some basic
facts of life that she has to tolerate. She needs to let her feet be touched and her nails cut.
(See Chapter 9.) She needs to allow the vet to examine her. She needs to greet humans
appropriately and respectfully. She should be taught all these things positively, of course,
but she should be taught them. You cannot capitulate to a Ridgeback's protests and simply
let her have her way. You will be creating a monster.

Photo: Denise Flaim

Chapter 7

Training Your Ridgeback

I keep saying that your Rhodesian Ridgeback is not a Labrador R[...]
more important to remember than in this chapter.

instructor seem rig[...]
does the instruct[...]
things.)

Don't
ch[...]

Many training classes are set up with "easy" breeds like Labs and Goldens in mind; reflexively obedient dogs like these want to please, and they get enjoyment from obeying their owners. In their case, the challenge is simply getting them to understand what you want.

Your Ridgeback has been bred for generations to do just the opposite: to think for himself and act accordingly. He will want to please you, but to a limit. Like a human, he will find the request to sit over and over again to be stupid. So in the Ridgeback's case, the challenge isn't just getting him to understand what you want – it's persuading him that he ought to do it, too.

Because they are so independent and bore so easily, Ridgebacks do not do well with monotonous or heavy-handed training techniques. If you think your dog-training class is boring, your Ridgeback will, too. Instead, he needs lots of positive motivation, lots of food and lots of variety.

Here's what you need to know to train your Ridgeback effectively, whether on your own, or in a group setting.

Puppy kindergarten is a must. As I said in the previous chapter, invest in a good puppy-kindergarten class for your new Ridgeback. Not only will she learn some basic obedience commands, but she will also learn how to be more confident in the world at large. Playing appropriately with other puppies her age and learning to navigate new experiences such as pee-wee-sized agility equipment will be valuable experiences that you simply cannot replicate once she leaves puppyhood behind.

Find a Ridgeback-savvy trainer. Many dog trainers have had little experience with independent breeds like Ridgebacks. They often mistake intelligence for obstinance and even stupidity. Inquire about how many "non-traditional" obedience breeds the instructor has worked with – say, Bulldogs, terriers and other hounds. If he starts telling you how dumb and headstrong Ridgebacks are, this is not the instructor for you.

Try before you buy. Before you join any training class, visit without your puppy and watch what is going on: Are the dogs praised profusely? Is food being used as a motivator and a reward? Are the dogs allowed to quit on a positive note? Do the instructors note breed differences and train accordingly? (All good things.)

Or do you see a lot of jerking of collars and harsh physical corrections? Does the

...d and harsh? Instead of respecting and working with breed differences, ...or dismiss certain independent breeds as "dumb" or "difficult"? (All bad

...ely on "remote" training. At some point during your tenure as a Ridgeback owner, ...nces are you'll be approached by a trainer who says he will take your dog for three ...weeks and return him a polished, obedient, respectful Ridgeback version of Lassie. *Run,* do not walk away from trainers like these.

Ridgebacks need to be trained by their owners, simple as that. That's not to say you shouldn't go to obedience class with an instructor who can guide and instruct you. But a Ridgeback does not have the temperament to be handed off to a complete stranger who will instill obedience into him. It just doesn't work that way. This is a sensitive and intelligent creature who understands the difference between a stranger and his people. He does not consider the humans in his life to be interchangeable. He will not accept – nor should he be expected to accept – orders from someone he doesn't know.

Don't zap your dog. You might be tempted to use an electronic collar – either because you've read about it or some enthusiastic trainer tells you it's the quickest and fastest and best way to get your Ridgeback to behave.

A puppy displaying "love ears." Ridgebacks hold their ears this way when they are feeling deferential or chagrinned. Learning to read your dog's body language will help immensely in training. *Photo: Jens Ratsey-Woodroffe*

Nothing could be further from the truth. It is tempting to think that a simple collar with a handheld controller could turn your Ridgeback into a robot who answers your every beck and call. But you didn't get a Ridgeback because you wanted a robot. You got a Ridgeback because the breed is intelligent, intuitive, sensitive, expansive – in short, you got this breed because it's as human as any dog gets.

I would no more use an electronic collar as my primary method of training a Ridgeback than I would use a cattle prod on my children to get them to be obedient.

And like children, Ridgebacks learn best through positive reinforcement. If they are zapped every time they make a mistake – and most of the time they won't even know what the mistake was – they will likely react in one of two ways: The will shut down, their

Learning "wait." If you have any doubt about a Ridgeback's food focus, this photo ought to dispel it! *Photo: Suzanne Humenik*

expressive, intelligent eyes going blank as they give up trying to understand what you're trying to teach them and becoming fearful of even making a move lest they invite another shock. Or they will react in self-defense, lashing out to defend themselves against what they see as an arbitrary and potentially life-threatening assault. Neither is a good outcome.

If you need a third party or someone with a shock collar to train your Ridgeback, then you are not equipped to have a Ridgeback in your life. It is as simple as that.

More is not always more. I have already said, incessantly, that Ridgebacks are very intelligent. As a result, they bore easily. You need to make sure that training sessions – and any new experiences, for that matter – are short and sweet and positive. Don't use other breeds as your yardstick. If you are in a training class filled with traditional Sporting breeds, chances are your Ridgeback is going to throw in the towel long before they even begin to tire. Quit when your Ridgeback is still eager to work for you. Don't feel that you have to keep up with everyone else. Your Ridgeback doesn't have to be drilled incessantly. It's very tempting when a Ridgeback has mastered something to try to go on to the very next thing. As tempting as it is to keep pushing through and keep on going, don't. Leave her wanting more.

Know when to ask for help. Sometimes it's hard to see the forest for the trees. Your dog might have a very simple issue that's easy to fix, but you're so immersed in the problem that you have no perspective. That's why it's important to have a network of Ridgeback-savvy people – hopefully with your breeder at the very top of the list – to turn to when you need advice, support and solutions. If for some reason you don't have access to your dog's breeder, and even if you don't know very many Ridgeback people, there are virtual Ridgeback communities where you can seek out help. The various Ridgeback groups on Facebook, the longstanding Ridgeback email list rr-folk (www.mandorichard.net/RR/list.html), Ridgeback owners who are also certified trainers – all can be great resources for you.

Ridgebacks love to bond to each other, but they are also acutely aware of how attention is shared by the humans in the household. Exploit this when training. *Photo: Denise Flaim*

Use high-value treats. If he's typical of the breed, your Ridgeback is highly food motivated – he'll bolt down anything that's not nailed down. But many owners forget that while a Milkbone in the kitchen may send your Ridgeback into spasms of ecstasy, that same everyday treat may seem less compelling in a new environment where there are exciting new sights and smells. The more distracting the environment, the more enticing, or "higher value," the treats must be. Beef jerky, cubed cheese, pieces of grilled chicken or steak … I knew a Ridgeback who lived for a piece of buttered bagel. (Messy, but very effective.) Use trial and error, and

see what really "turns your Ridgeback on." The more excited she is
more enthusiastic she will be about training.

Harness the power of jealousy. Ridgebacks hate to be left out. They'
what's going on around them in their households, and they have a d
he got and I didn't. If you're lucky enough to own two Ridgebacks (o
a housemate of any other breed), utilize them against each other.

You can put a lea
bucking, resis
collar, he'
stairs
str

In training class, if my Ridgeback starts ignoring me and sniffing the floor, turning his
nose up at my treats and me, I simply give him a verbal cue, "That's it, you blew it," and
he gets put back in his crate. Then I start working with another dog, right in front of
him, cooing and praising the other dog profusely. Jealousy is a powerful motivator in this
breed; use it to your advantage.

When you train, always have one dog crated (or in a down-stay, when your puppy is well
trained enough to consistently comply). Trying to train two Ridgebacks simultaneously is
just going to end up in a lot of confusion.

Positive, positive, positive. Your Ridgeback learns best through positive experiences and
interactions. He does not do well by you showing him what he's done wrong. Instead, he
wants to know and flourishes by knowing what he's done right. Jerk-and-pop training,
where you use correction and compulsion to "teach" the dog, is doomed to failure with a
Ridgeback.

Of course, sometimes you will need to be firm with your Ridgeback, and sometimes
punishment might be required. How do you tell when that is the case? For me, the
distinction is whether or not the Ridgeback understands she is breaking the rules. If she is
genuinely frightened, confused or apprehensive, then coercion will make matters worse.
If, however, she knows you don't want her jumping on the counter, or stealing your salami
sandwich, then your firm rebuke will be met in the spirit of understanding – though she
still won't be happy about it.

Outthinking Your Ridgeback

if dog starts growling w/ food

You cannot force a Ridgeback to do what he does not want to do. Instead, you need to find
a way to motivate him to do it.

The best way to get a reluctant Ridgeback to do something is to trick him into thinking it's
his idea. This is a lot easier than it sounds.

Let's say you want your Ridgeback to go into the basement. Let's also say that your
Ridgeback thinks this is a supremely bad idea, because there are demonic forces lurking
under the stairs.

You can do one of two things in this scenario:

...sh on your dog, and drag him down the stairs, which will result in him ...ing and planting his feet on the ground. Chances are once you release his ...bolt right back up the stairs. And the next time you try to bring him down the ...'ll either hide himself on the opposite end of the house or give you an even bigger ...ggle, escalating to the point where he might even feel compelled to protect himself. Keep going in this direction, and I see a dog bite on your horizon.

Or you can do what I do: Don't feed him that morning (an otherwise normal and healthy Ridgeback can afford to miss a meal) and leave a delicious piece of cheese on each step leading down to the basement. If he doesn't take the bait, don't feed him at night, either, and try again. Eventually, your Ridgeback will want to go into the basement.

Your Ridgeback might only go down one step or two, and then beat a hasty retreat. He might not go down at all, instead pacing and whining in front of the stairs, vocalizing his frustration and indecision. That's fine; leave the basement door open with the treats in place, and eventually your Ridgeback is going to find his way down. He might not do it in the first session. It might take a few tries. Maybe instead of the cheese, you'll need to put his food bowl on one of the steps. But when he's hungry– that is to say, motivated – enough, he'll eventually consider a trip to the basement worth his while.

A similar scenario works with Ridgebacks who get growly when anyone approaches their food bowl while they're eating. (Of course, any Ridgeback who gives signals that he even potentially might cross the line and bite needs to be seen by a certified behaviorist. *Do not* attempt this if you feel your dog poses any potential to react aggressively to you.) As your Ridgeback is eating his regular dinner, fill your hand with some outrageously delicious treat that he loves. Don't skimp: Try marinated steak or grilled chicken breast or even a slice of pizza. Standing near him, drop the treats into the bowl. If you are using the right kind of treat, he'll be pleasantly surprised.

Continue doing this at every mealtime. Eventually, he'll be eager to see you approach. Then you can place the treats in your hand and slide them into the bowl so he can eat them out of your hand. (Again, if you have any concern that putting your hand near the bowl will result in a bite, don't attempt this. Rather, seek out a professional trainer.) Once he's happy and comfortable with that, you can practice taking the bowl away mid-meal, giving him a lavish treat, and then returning the bowl. In this way he learns that your approach, that your hands making their way toward his bowl, all mean good things. He learns that in the end letting you touch and even take away his food means he gets more.

You see the pattern in these two examples: You don't use coercion to get the Ridgeback to do what you want to do. In fact it's quite the opposite: You set up situations where the Ridgeback actually thinks he's decided to do what you want.

Clicker Training

When it comes to training, there's arguably no approach that's more exciting and effective with Ridgebacks than clicker training. Once you understand what it is, clicker training

is quite simple. But it requires a little bit of thought to get the basic concepts under your belt.

A clicker is just a handheld device that makes a crisp "click" sound when you press it. Once hard to find, they are now readily available at chain stores such as Petco.

A lot of people think clickers are like remote controls. You click and the dog does what you want, sort of like changing the channel from PBS to ESPN. But that's not it at all. The clicker is a marker. In other words it's a neutral sound that never varies that marks, or points out, what the dog is doing that you like. So if you want your dog to chase his tail and you click when he's doing that, you're using the clicker correctly. Now it's a little more complicated than that, because the dog needs to understand what the click means, and your timing has to be just right, but that's really the general idea. If you see it, and you like it, click it.

Ridgeback puppies learning the "watch me" command. This is very easy to teach with clicker training.
Photo: Jens Ratsey-Woodroffe

As we've discussed before, Ridgebacks love it when things are their idea. Once your dog understands how the clicker works, he understands that he is the one who's driving the process. In other words, you're not clicking to make him do something; instead, he's doing something to make you click. He is the one in control, and Ridgebacks love that.

Once your dog understands the clicker is, and he sees you take it out, you'll see him enthusiastically offer all kinds of behaviors in an effort to get you to click. This kind of enthusiasm in training Ridgeback is often very difficult to solicit with traditional training.

But with the clicker, it just comes naturally.

Many professional trainers use clicker training as their main teaching approach. If you can't find a clicker class near you, ask your obedience instructor if you can use the clicker in your regular class, provided the noise of the clicker does not distract other owners.

The ABCs of Clicking

Here's a step-by-step introduction to this very effective – and fun! – training approach:

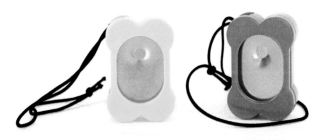

"Charge" the clicker. Before you begin clicking training, your Ridgeback needs to understand what the clicker is, and what a click means. "Charging" the clicker means showing the dog exactly that.

Clickers are inexpensive and available at most chain pet stores. *Photo: Dreamstime*

Here's how you do that: Get some treats that your dog really loves and your clicker. Go to a room in your house where there aren't many distractions. Simply click the clicker and then give your dog a treat. Click, treat. Click, treat. That's it.

Make sure your Ridgeback is enthusiastic about the treat; if she's not, you may have to wait a few hours until she is a bit hungrier, or switch to something she likes better.

No rat-a-rat-ratting. The rule is one click, one treat – no multiple clicks. Every time the dog hears a click, she must receive a treat. This is the contract that you are signing with your Ridgeback: A click means a treat is coming.

Keep this introduction to the clicker relatively short – a minute or two, say 10 to 15 clicks, should be enough for the first session. You can try having a number of these sessions a day. Usually by the third or fourth session, the Ridgeback begins to understand that when you take out the clicker, you're going to click, and when you click, he's going to get a treat. And chances are pretty good you'll have his full attention.

If your dog is really into it, wait a few minutes until she turns her head or goes to start sniffing the floor. When that happens, click. If your dog is beginning to associate the sound of the click with food, she'll probably whip around or look up at you. It's working!

A word about talking: Don't. You don't need to augment the clicker with any kind of verbal praise. The click is powerful enough. It tells the dog that's it and now the treat is coming. Talking during the process only confuses things. Just let the clicker do its work.

Remember that the click stops the behavior. Let's say you're teaching your dog how to sit. You get your timing just right and click just as your dog's rear meets the floor. When he hears the click, he will jump up in anticipation of his treat. This is not a problem. What a dog hears the click, he expects his treat. It's perfectly okay for him to do so.

Pick one thing to teach. Once you've "charged" the clicker, it's time to start training. I like to start out with "Watch me." For this you're clicking each time the dog's eyes meet yours. Chances are it won't be too hard to have your dog meet your eyes, even for just half a second.

The second the dog makes eye contact with you, click, and then give a treat. Don't say anything, just click and treat. Your timing is hugely important with the clicker: You have to click at the exact moment the dog's eyes meet yours. If you don't click just as he looks at you, you'll click his looking away. (Even if you make a timing mistake, he gets the treat.)

Give the behavior a name. When you are teaching your dog what you're clicking for – that is, when he's still figuring out just what it is that you want from him – you don't use any words at all. You let the clicker talk for you.

Once, however, your Ridgeback begins offering the behavior that you're clicking for consistently – let's say he stares at you for five or 10 seconds straight – then you can give it a name. Tell your dog "Watch me," and when he looks at you, click only after you say the words and he looks – that is, if he's looking at you trying to get you to click, don't. You only click if this sequence happens: While he's looking away, you say, "Watch me," and then he makes eye contact with you.

When your Ridgeback understand the "watch me" command, you can get more selective in your clicking. You may only decide to click after he stares at you for three seconds, then four seconds, then five. The idea is to keep upping the ante: The more your Ridgeback

Most Ridgebacks find traditional obedience to be too rigid. (And it's tough to get them to retrieve those dumbbells!) Most consider agility (far right), with its fast pace, to be much more appealing.
Photos: Dreamstime

understands what you want, the more you refine what you're asking for.

"Fade the clicker." Eventually, the clicker is "faded" from the command; that is, you don't need it anymore, since the purpose of the clicker is only to teach a command. You use it to say, "Yes! That! The thing you did right then!" And once the dog understand what "that" is, the clicker has done its job.

The whole point behind clicker training is – you don't make the dog do something; you wait until he does it, then click it. This makes the dog think it's *his* idea, not yours, that somehow he is in control, that he is making *you* click. And the enthusiasm level is awesome.

If I sit on the living-room couch with my clicker and a bag of treats, my dogs will sit in front of me and literally go through the entire repertoire of things they know, trying to figure out how to get me to click. It's amazing to watch them *think*.

Another advantage of the clicker is it allows you to pinpoint specific behavior. The second you click – that is the thing being rewarded. There is no doubt in the dog's mind about what he did right. It also allows you to teach things you couldn't possibly do with a traditional approach. My first female Ridgeback, Diva, always plastered her ears to the side of her head in the show ring. I taught the command "Ears" by clicking when she was alert and her ears were set nicely forward. Whenever I said "Ears," she reflexively perked them.

I also used the clicker to teach Diva the seesaw at agility class. She hated the loud *boom* it made, and didn't want to go near it. So at first I clicked her looking at it. Then I clicked her going toward it. Then I clicked her putting one foot on it while I lured her toward it with some food. Then I clicked two feet, etc. Throughout her lifetime, given a choice of a whole ring full of agility equipment, she gravitated toward the seesaw because she associated it with such positive things.

Seek serendipity. Sometimes when you're trying to teach your dog one behavior, he'll inadvertently offer you another that is so cute you can't help but click it. That's the cool thing about clicker-training: It's spontaneous, it's organic, and it can take you unexpected places. If your dog offers you a behavior that you didn't ask for, don't be so rigid and say to yourself, "But we were not training *that* – we were training *this*!" Be willing to take the detour, because you might not get that opportunity again. When it comes to Ridgebacks, everything is about flexibility.

One great example of this is tail chasing. Ridgeback puppies will often chase their tails for the sheer joy of it. If you are quick enough, you can click this behavior while your dog's in the middle of it. Of course, your Ridgeback will stop doing that and right away come to get his treat. He might not go back to tail chasing again right away – he may not make the connection. But if you manage to click two or three different times, chances are he'll begin to understand that's what gets clicked. And then you'll have a whirling dervish of a Ridgeback, just waiting for you to click again.

Appreciate the "good" mistakes. The fascinating thing about clicker training is that sometimes your dog thinks you're looking for something entirely different. For example if you're clicking for "Watch me," and he happens to blink just as you click, he might very well think

Clicker-training makes it easy to "capture" behaviors, like this full-body stretch ("Take a bow"). *Photo: Denise Flaim*

you're clicking for blinking. In cases such as these, you can either ignore the blinking and wait until he stares before you click, or you can decide to click for the blinking. Since it's tougher to get a Ridgeback to blink than to stare, I'd go for the former.

Once he learned that blink behavior, and you give it a name, then you can go on and teach "Watch." That's what's so great about clicker training: The possibilities are endless.

Where the Wild Things Are

When you have an animal that's too large or too dangero[us] killer whale or cheetah – clicker training is the way to go. and zookeepers use clicker training to teach these animals to perform. The effects of clicker training are lasting because compulsion to make the animal do what you want her to do. the tools to understand what you want, and then give her a mo

In the same way, clicker training is a great way to capture behavio couldn't manipulate your dog into doing. Here are some tricks and that you can teach easily with clicker training:

"Leave It." Put a delicious treat in the palm of your hand, then close your fist around it. Present your closed fist to your Ridgeback, who will in all likelihood sniff it. Don't open your fist. Eventually, your dog will get frustrated and turn her head away from your fist. At that precise moment, click, then open your fist and give her the treat. Repeat that several times. Soon, your dog will realize that by leaving the treat alone, she'll get it.

"Take a bow." You know this maneuver – your dog extends his front legs out in front of him and sticks his rear in the air so he can get a nice, long, good stretch. The best time to capture this behavior is when he's gotten up from a good night's sleep or nap. Click at the precise moment that his front legs are most extended and his rear is highest up in the air.

"Stir it." Basically, this is tail chasing on command. Ridgeback puppies usually will chase their tails before they start growing up to be serious adolescents. If you have your clicker handy you can click and mark this behavior, and very soon have it on cue.

"Sing." Ridgebacks are sometimes inspired to howl when there's an ambulance siren in the distance or when they hear a wolf vocalizing on some PBS documentary. Again, if you have your clicker handy, you can click to capture that behavior. If after the first time you have trouble getting your dog to repeat the howling, just do a little howling yourself. Oftentimes, your fake howls are enough to prompt him start doing it.

Chapter 8

Kids and Ridgebacks

Some of the very earliest photos we have of Ridgebacks on the farms and encampments of Rhodesia in the early part of the 20th Century show them in the company of children. This isn't an accident: Ridgebacks have a deep affinity for "their" children, and are much more tolerant of them than many other more short-tempered breeds.

That said, as with any new experience, Ridgeback puppies need frequent, positive exposure to children and their accoutrements, like baby carriages and bouncers, in order to feel comfortable around them. Even if you don't have children now, or have no intention of acquiring any in the future, some of your friends and family likely do. Exposing your puppy to well-behaved children, always being careful to supervise the interactions, will hard-wire him to associated diminutive humans with pleasant things.

First impressions with Ridgebacks are hugely important, and nothing is more important than ensuring puppies are comfortable as well as safe around their inquisitive human counterparts.

Kids and dogs are a lot of work: Both can make spectacular messes if not supervised, and it takes a lot of time to raise them properly. They bring to the surface all your shortcomings, as the crunch of bringing them up makes you confront old patterns and programming.

But their mutual gift is their visceral delight in the world that many of us adults lost sight of long ago. When you watch the relationship between a child and her dog – the whispered confidences, the gleeful playbowing, the sheer joy of running in the grass together – you rediscover what it's all about.

And as the Ridgebacks turn gray and then white and then are no more, I don't have any better explanation for the children than the one I give myself: The old dogs leave to make room for the new ones to follow, to give us a fresh infusion of joy and wonder at this marvelous, unfolding miracle called life.

Which Should Come First?

To be honest, there is no good answer to this "chicken and egg" question. Kids first, Ridgeback first – they both have their pros and cons.

If you have the children first, then a new Ridgeback puppy will have no issues bonding to and accepting them. But if you have the Ridgeback first, then you have a chance to enjoy her fully, learn her quirks and idiosyncrasies, and strengthen the relationship for the challenges that come with kids and an expanding household.

Young children must be taught proper handling. *Photo: ThruMarzenasLens.com*

Another advantage to bringing kids into a household with Ridgebacks already present is the immune-system benefit. Studies show that children who grow up with dogs (and cats) are less likely to develop asthma and allergies to a wide variety of allergens, but – here's the clincher – exposure during the child's first year of life is key. After that, the preventive benefits are severely decreased.

Many Ridgeback breeders are not comfortable selling to families with toddlers or preschoolers. This has less to do with the puppy, and more to do with the child: Ridgebacks are notoriously boisterous puppies, and by the time most children are five years or older, they are better able to handle the nipping, chasing and toy demolishing that is part and parcel of a puppy's arrival in the household.

Older Ridgebacks and New Babies

When Stephen, Allie and Krista came into my life – in that order, a couple of minutes apart – I had two middle-aged Ridgebacks. Blitz and Diva had certainly met children before, and didn't mind them, but the arrival of my triplets rocked their world. Pre-kids, my husband Fred and I went to work, and they lazed around our suburban Victorian, maybe getting exorcised over the occasional oil delivery or Fed Ex dropoff. But post-kids, there was a literal village tromping through the house – grandmothers, babysitters, a visiting aunt from Italy – and these, these … *creatures*.

Diva, an old hand at motherhood herself, decided avoidance was the best option: Anytime I sat down next to her with a baby in my arms, and a tightly balled fist or bootied foot grazed her, she got up without so much as a sidelong glance and, well, left.

Blitz, on the other hand, was a basket case. Like many intact males, he had what one behaviorist I talked to eloquently called Old Bachelor Uncle Syndrome. He reacted to my newborn children the same way he did to newly whelped puppies presented under his nose for inspection: "Uh, what are these things? Ew, they smell weird. I thought I wanted to know, but – actually – no … " *Backing away … backing away …*

When my triplets started to toddle, he looked at them whale-eyed, just as he did with puppies barreling around the room, running in between his legs, millipedes with fur: "What are these things? They still smell weird. Is one of them going to grab my testicles?"

(A prophetic concern, as you will see.) *Growling ... growling ...*

It was a little unnerving having a 90-pound intact male Ridgeback vibrating like a tuning fork around my little swathed bundles of pinkness. But with my favorite remedy – tincture of time – and some hard-earned experience, we eventually overcame his reluctance. That first year of mixing dogs and babies was stressful, but it taught me more than any "What to Expect ..." book could.

In fact, nobody really tells you what to expect when you bring a new baby home to an older dog. The advice books tell you what to do to prepare your dog for the arrival, but there's not much information about how to prepare yourself for what happens when things get a little bumpy.

Ridgebacks are consummate family dogs, and once mine recalibrated their definition of our family, we were in for smooth sailing. My babies were foreign things to Blitz until, over time, he came to realize they were ours. Once he understood that, he became their dear friend, their protector.

Some tips to keep in mind:

The advice books are only a starting point. Yes, do the whole blanket-from-the-hospital shtick. Walk around the house with a doll and talk mindlessly to it. But Ridgebacks are smart. They know the doll isn't a baby. They know that everything in their world is changing: As your pregnancy progresses, everything about you starts to morph, from your gait to your hormones to your routine. New furniture shows up. Rooms get rearranged. Your anxiety level peaks.

Any major change in your life requires an adjustment period, and dogs are no different.

Photo: Denise Flaim

Just assume that this will be the case, and provide your Ridgeback with the space – both mental and physical – to figure things out. When things get hectic, or out of control, give her crate time with a good chewie. Don't expect the Normal Rockwell painting out of the gate; for the first few months, it may be more paint by numbers.

Listen to the dog people. Babies and kids make people emotional – no way of getting around that. Fledgling grandmothers who in other aspects of their lives are unflappable turn into frantic Oracles of Delphi when your Ridgeback so much as looks at the new arrival.

Illustration: Allie Eder

Amid all the confusion and exhaustion of a new baby, it's easy to let other people get into your head. If it's an experienced dog person, that's one thing. But if it's someone whose sum total exposure to canines is a collection of German bisque Dachshunds, then keep that in perspective. People who understand dogs understand canine body language; people who don't are liable to misinterpret even friendly gestures – "He's LICKING HER! Oh, my God, HE'S LICKING HER!" – and can offer some rather insane advice.

Last week, on a visit to the periodontist, the chairside chatter turned to the assistant's newborn granddaughter, who was coming home from the hospital later that week. Concerned that the family dog was not going to accept the baby readily, the plan was to tranquilize him. I almost swallowed my cotton batting, and when I could come up for air I pointed out that this was a supremely bad idea; in fact, being woozy and out of control of his own body likely would put the dog *more* on edge, not less.

Center yourself. Dogs read your body language, your pheromones – and, the animal communicators would say, your thoughts. If you are anxious and worried about your Ridgeback's reaction to the baby, you are in a sense encouraging him to be. Find that sweet spot between vigilant and freaked out. Practice feeling it. Practice breathing normally and not holding your breath when the two are in the room together – that's the first sign to your dog that there is something to be worried about.

Don't run film loops in your head about the worst-case scenarios. Do try to envision a calm, serene encounter. This sounds simple, and in theory it is, but in practice it can be the most daunting hurtle you face, especially if you have a dog who's having difficulty with the new-baby transition.

Take baby steps. The most important thing to remember with anything involving dogs, or kids – or dogs and kids together – is that you can't expect a finished product right out of the gate. Plan out your encounters between dog and child – no matter what the age – and start simple: Create tiny successes and build from there.

In my Blitz's case, he exhibited a spectrum of emotions, starting first with excitement, leaping and snuffing. When he smelled the babies through the bars of the crib, he breathed their scent in so deeply he sounded like an Electrolux. Once the novelty wore off, and the babies became a fixed part of our routine, then bewilderment set in. He was fine as long as they didn't touch him. Once they did, the panicked looks and grumbling started.

We dealt with his behavior in a number of ways. To help center his emotions gently and without drugs, I added some appropriate flower essences to his water, like Walnut for dramatic life changes, Mimulus for fear and Rescue Remedy to kick it up a notch. (In my experience, when I have found the individual essences that work, adding Rescue Remedy often amplifies their results.) Whenever Blitz was around the babies and reacted without fear or concern, he'd get a click and a treat.

Corrections don't work when fear or anxiety is at the root of the problem; they only make things worse. But if I did hear a grumble when I sat beside Blitz on the couch with a baby and bottle, he was calmly but firmly ejected from his spot.

Photo: ThruMarzenasLens.com

Fast forward five or so years later. Blitz was sleeping in the front parlor; my baby sitter was playing a boisterous game of tag with the kids, chasing them around the kitchen island. When their delighted screams reached his ears, he bounced off the couch, trotted over to the babysitter, and took her forearm gently between his powerful jaws. She stopped, the kids' screaming died down, and he released her, without so much as a tooth mark. Rather than being taken aback, she was pleased: He was telling her, eloquently but wordlessly, that he was worried about his children, and she needed to stop their screaming. Now.

When those babies first came home, I would have never thought that scenario possible. But dogs, like people, just need an adjustment period.

Training the Human Puppies

Now the opposite scenario: Ridgeback puppies who go into a household with children.

I am going to try to say this in a way that does not offend, but if you take exception to it, maybe you need to look a little more closely at your child rearing: I can tell how a Ridgeback puppy will turn out by looking at how the family's children behave.

Children who visit a breeder's house and have no self-control, venturing into distant rooms without being invited, touching delicate items high up on shelves, basically running around like banshees, are an excellent predictor that their parents will raise a pushy, out-of-control and manner-less Ridgeback.

This isn't the child's fault, or the Ridgeback's, for that matter: The blame lies squarely with the parents, who failed to instill a sense of boundaries, appropriateness and self-control.

Just as dogs need to be trained, so do children. Teach them that the crate is totally off limits to anyone with two legs: This is the dog's sanctuary, a place where he can retreat and be assured that no one will pester him.

At the earliest age, you can begin to teach the fundamentals of respecting animals and

100

their boundaries. A staple around our house was "Tails Are Not for Pulling" by Elizabeth Verdick, whose title is a handy catch phrase to repeat when a yank of any body part looks imminent.

With my kids, however, the anatomy did not generalize. One day I found 3-year-old Allie crouched beside Blitz, who was sprawled out on his side. As I walked by, Allie reached out to Blitz, who jerked his head up suddenly, then sighed and dropped it to the ground, resigned.

Photo: ThruMarzenasLens.com

"What did you do?" I asked Allie, who looked very pleased with herself.

"I squeezed his butt," she announced proudly, pointing at his testicles.

That occasioned an impromptu "Testicles Are Not for Tugging" discussion, which in turn led to an exploration of physiological gender differences. (That's the great thing about having dogs: Being naked all the time, they are great springboards for the "birds and bees" discussions that make some adults so very nervous.)

Ridgeback puppies are by nature boisterous and, especially when they are teething, mouthy. If you have a child who is very sensitive, and will not be able to good-naturedly shrug off the occasional puppy jump or nip (after you have intercepted it or redirected it, which is your job as the adult), then reconsider getting a puppy. Children need to understand that puppies are babies themselves, and it will take some time for them to learn what is expected of them. In the process, they might be inadvertently jostled or mouthed, and they are just going to have to learn to cope with it (proactively, of course, such as redirecting the puppy's mouthing to an appropriate toy).

At every age, kids have questions about their interactions with the family dog, and you need to keep your antennae primed for them. When he was eight, my son Stephen woefully informed me that our newest puppy no longer liked him because she was nipping at him. When I told Stephen that Gigi was getting mouthy because she had been playing with her visiting brother, and dogs wrestle with their mouths just as he and his sisters do with their hands, he broke into a big grin. Gigi not only liked him, he realized; she was trying to play with him.

As I said in an earlier chapter, one of the first things my kids learned was the directive "Seek higher ground." This is useful when they are nibbling on a cheese stick and are surrounded by a throng of red fur; standing on the couch, mozzarella held aloft like Lady Liberty's torch, they have a chance at keeping it. But the "higher ground" mantra also works when two dogs are playing and the action looks intense, or when a new dog comes over and is introduced into the pack. The children are made to understand that when there is a lot of excitement among the dogs, they need to get out of the way, lest they get mixed up and inadvertently hurt if things escalate.

Another thing they learned was how their behavior could elicit unwanted reactions from the dogs. If they squealed and ran, chances are the new puppy would pursue, and seek to engage them with those pin-sharp baby teeth. They learned how to rebuke puppy nips by offering a toy, and, as they got older, how to dissuade a humper. (Issue a loud, deep, "NO!" and bop on the head, more than once if necessary. I'm all for positive reinforcement, but when I have a 90-pound male Ridgeback looking for a hormone hug with a 70-pound second-grader, we do what works. And that works.)

Harness the Helpfulness

Younger children love to be helpers, and mine vied to do even the most mundane tasks: stuffing Kongs with peanut butter; wetting, wringing and freezing washcloths when teething was going full tilt; filling the water bowl up – and up, and up … .

(Because I feed raw, I wouldn't let the children help with mealtime. And until they were four or so, I cooked the dogs' food, because I was worried about cross-contamination. The kids learned to ask, "Have the dogs eaten yet?" which was a signal they were debating whether to permit a doggie kiss on the lips. Our home rule is no face contact for one hour after the dogs have eaten.)

When I have a litter, I could not ask for better puppy socializers. My kids are in the whelping box constantly. They delight in handling the puppies, naming them, noting their differences in appearance and temperament. They are never there unsupervised, and have been taught to be gentle; if they break any rule, they lose their "box privileges." This results in puppies who are programmed to love little kids; as adult dogs, when they see a little human, even on the horizon, their bodies waggle and wiggle in delight.

Remember, though, that kids, like dogs, are individuals. My youngest daughter, Krista, could take the dogs, or leave them. I suspect both nature and nurture have a hand in being "doggie": Some kids are just more drawn to these furry folk than others, and that's OK.

Reality Check

As Allie's aforementioned game of tug demonstrates, potentially dangerous situations between kids and dogs happen. Even the best-behaved child disobeys now and then. I was fortunate to have a well-temperamented dog with a high tolerance about his personal space among his "pack."

Several years back, I covered a tragic story for the newspaper that I worked for at the time. A little girl had been strangled to death in the backyard by the family Golden Retriever. The dog was playing tug with her scarf – it was a complete freak accident. I interviewed experts and behaviorists, one of whom announced definitively that parents should ensure that children and dogs are never left unsupervised. I asked if she had kids. Of course, she didn't.

If you have kids, you know that sometimes it's just unavoidable to leave the two species together

Photo: ThruMarzenasLens.com

– if only for a minute to run some laundry to the basement, or check the dinner on the stove. Life happens. Constant supervision is the ideal, but sometimes you just can't be in control of everything. That's not resignation – that's reality.

And the vast majority of the time, things go absolutely perfectly. But then there are those rare, tragic events that remind us that there are two parts to the term "companion dog." Love them as we do, these are animals, with sharp teeth and instincts that we sometimes cannot predict. Always err on the side of caution. You do both your children and your dog a favor in being as conservative as possible, and supervising as much as you can, especially with visiting children in the house. When in doubt, use the crate. A bell cannot be unrung, an egg cannot be unscrambled – and some "mistakes" on the part of an otherwise stable and loving dog can exact a heavy toll.

Chapter 9

Ears and Nails

It might seem odd to devote a whole chapter to these two body parts. But if there are any aspects of the canine bodyscape that give new Ridgeback owners trouble, these are the two. And they tend to be the most overlooked by novices, who do not think to pay attention to them until it is too late.

Flying Ears

Maybe you're old enough to have watched "The Flying Nun," a television show starring Sally Field as Sister Bertrille, a novice nun who, as the show's title suggests, was able to take to the air. This was due to her cornette, or headgear, which was so heavily starched and folded that it looked like a piece of origami.

When a Ridgeback puppy begins teething (usually around four months, sometimes earlier) and later, when the back molars are cut, she, too, can develop "flying nun ears." Instead of lying flat like great big triangles, the ears begin to fold and crimp. At the same time, the feet may also go flat.

Sometimes, this begins subtly: The ears may curl slightly instead of tightly framing the face. Or they may lift at the spot where they fold to meet the head, forming the beginnings of what is called a "button ear." This is desirable in a Fox Terrier – but not a Ridgeback!

Who cares if your Ridgeback's ears start to misbehave? *You* should care: Because if you do not correct them, they will stay that way. You might not notice or care now. But as you grow to know the breed, and understand how a nice, flat ear adds a beautiful frame to the head, you will have wished you had taken care of this cosmetic concern. (And to be sure, it is cosmetic: Your Ridgeback will not care what his ears look like, and there are no negative health implications from having a less-than-perfectly hanging ear.)

Above: Sally Field's signature "Flying Nun" habit. Below: A Ridgeback's convincing impression.

Photos: Dreamstime

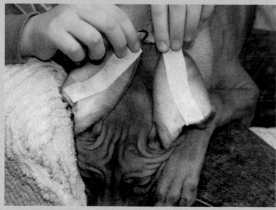

Gather your supplies: Rubbing alcohol, first-aid tape (waterproof is ideal), cotton balls and blunt-end scissors.

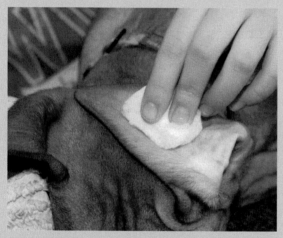

Clean the ear flap, removing oil so the tape sticks well.

Apply the strips of tape to each ear.

Photos: ThruMarzenasLens.com

How to Tape Ears

Each Ridgeback breeder has her own way of ear taping. But the principle is the same: Waterproof first-aid tape (the wider, the better) is used to secure the ears in the desired position. It can take only a few days or as much as a week for the ears to return to normal; this usually coincides with the tape falling off!

If by some miracle the tape stays on for longer than a week, remove it and see how the ears look. Even if they appear to need more taping, leave the ears untaped for a day, then retape. Allowing air to circulate will help avoid ear infections.

• Use rubbing alcohol to clear the inside flaps of your puppy's ears. (*Not* inside the ear: Just the surface of the ear flap.) Don't stint on this step: Be sure to rub thoroughly. You are trying to remove as much oil as possible so that the tape you're going to add next attaches firmly. (When a Danish breeder I was visiting wanted me to show her how to tape ears, there was no rubbing alcohol in the house. We found that schnapps works in a pinch!)

• Wait until the rubbing alcohol dries thoroughly before proceeding to the next step: Flip your puppy's ear flap over again and roughly measure the length of the ear flap, from the opening of the ear to the tip of the flap. If you have a good eye, you can eyeball this; the measurement doesn't have to be exact.

• Cut two pieces of first-aid tape to this length. Again, flip one ear flap over and secure one of the tape pieces to the inside of the flap, so that it runs parallel to the length of the ear, ending at the ear tip. Repeat on the other ear. If you have excess length, allow it to overlap the ear tip, NOT the opening to the ear.

These pieces of tape will be the "bases" to which you attach another, longer piece of tape that will connect them.

• Cut a piece of tape to double the length of one of the strips that you just cut. Carefully, taking care not to tangle it, attach the sticky side of this long piece of tape to one of the pieces of tape on the under-flap of one ear. Holding that ear tight to the puppy's head, run the remaining tape under the puppy's chin, and attach it to the tape on the underside of the other ear. Be sure that the ears are held taut against the head; if you have excess tape on the long piece, carefully cut it (use blunt-edge scissors to avoid accidents with a wriggly puppy!), or start anew with a smaller piece.

• To ensure the tape is well secured, tamp the each ear between your thumb and fingers, pressing gently.

• At the end of this process, you should have no tape visible, and your annoyed puppy will look like her ears are forming a tight bonnet around her head.

• For added security, I sometimes add another piece of tape on the outside of the ears, running it from the top of one ear, under the chin, and over to the flap of the other ear.

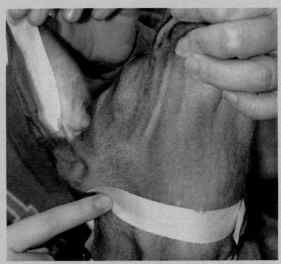

Attach the long piece of tape to the underside of one ear, so it sticks to the tape you secured there. In this photo, the longer tape's sticky side is facing the camera.

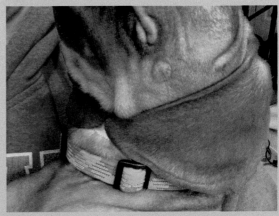

Repeat on other side. When done, the ears should almost resemble a bonnet.

For added security, you can add a piece of tape on the outside of the ears.

"Flying ears" result from the heavy calcium demands on a puppy's body during teething. Calcium deficiencies can weaken cartilage, and in puppyhood we see evidence of this in the ear cartilage, which begins to lose its firmness.

An ear intervention, in progress: Top left, ears gone wild, looking more Fox Terrier (top right) than Ridgeback! Below left, ears taped. Below right, untaped ears back to normal.

Giving additional calcium in natural form (whole milk, egg shells, cottage cheese) can often help remedy this situation. Because milk products can cause diarrhea in dogs, give them only to bowel tolerance: If you see that the stool is loosening, cut back on the amount of dairy you are giving.

If a puppy's "flyaway" ears do not resolve with calcium supplementation within a week or so, they must be taped; otherwise they will "freeze" in this position and cannot be undone. You only have a

At first glance, the ears of the puppy at right look fine, but there are telltale signs of an impending Sally Field moment: The corners of the ears, where they attach to the head, are beginning to lift, and the sides of the ear flaps are pulling away from the face. At minimum, this is a sign to up the calcium in the diet by adding whole milk to each meal.

Photos: Karen Dindial (ear progression); Dreamstime (Wire Fox Terrier) and Eileen Eisenhower (right)

brief window to deal with this before it becomes permanent – do not delay! Beyond the age of five or six months, the damage is irreversible.

Nail Trimming

If there is one Waterloo for Ridgeback owners, it is nail cutting. Most Ridgebacks innately and intensely dislike having their nails cut. They react as if amputation is imminent.

Guillotine-style nail clippers are often disastrous with Ridgebacks; the pressure from the blade seems to unnerve them. Another disadvantage with these clippers is since Ridgeback nails are usually black, you are often unable to avoid the "quick," or the blood supply to the nail. (Ridgebacks with white on their feet will often have lighter-colored nails, which are transparent enough for you to see the little line that is the quick.) Inadvertently cutting the quick is painful and bloody, and it only takes one time before your Ridgeback concludes that, again, you are trying your level best to kill him.

By contrast, Ridgebacks seem to do much better with having their nails ground instead of clipped. (More on that below.) This is probably because the grinder will not suddenly cut the quick, and will give you time to stop before you draw blood.

But no matter how you cut nails, your Ridgeback probably won't like it at first. You're going to have to be persistent and overcome her objections. This is not something she is going to like, and something she will go to great lengths to avoid.

You cannot – I repeat, *cannot* – permit your Ridgeback to set the parameters and rules about nail cutting. Simply put, if given the choice, your Ridgeback will not permit you to do it. Long, unkempt nails are not only unattractive,

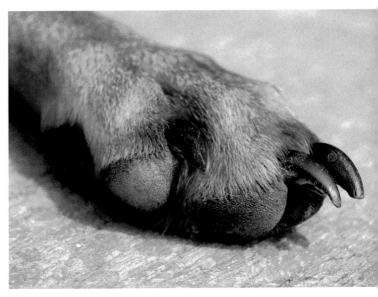

Grind nails once week to avoid them getting overly long and curved, as these are. *Photo: Dreamstime/Anke van Wyk*

but they damage floors, can severely scratch or injure you, and can impede the dog's locomotion, to the point where they destroy the shape of his foot.

The key to being successful in cutting your dog's nails is to just continue to do it on a regular basis after you bring him home at eight weeks old. When he is a small puppy, he may scream and retract his paw, but with a little encouragement and a lot of treats, he will soon come to accept this – especially if he realizes he has no choice. But show a little weakness, and it's all over.

Dremeling Nails

In order to grind a Ridgeback's nails, you need a Dremel – one of those hand-held rotary tools sold at Home Depot and other home-improvements stores. I don't bother with the battery-powered Dremel – it doesn't have enough juice. Go with the plug-in and use the cylindrical, sandpaper-covered sanding attachment.

Many Ridgebacks respond positively to this method of nail maintenance if properly introduced. This involves gradually introducing the tool, which is loud and vibrates strongly, both factors that can initially unnerve your Ridgeback.

Start with your Dremel unplugged, and a pile of cubed cheese at your side. Tap the Dremel gently against your puppy's nail. Treat generously and repeat many times.

Once your dog is more interested in the cheese than the Dremel, plug the Dremel in, but do not apply it to the nails yet! Your Ridgeback will likely be alarmed by the sound it makes. Turn the Dremel on in short bursts, giving treats generously after each one, until your dog is more interested in the cheese than the sound of the Dremel. (If you are really ambitious, you can turn the Dremel on as "background noise" whenever the puppy is eating. This will quickly desensitize her to it.)

Once your puppy is comfortable with the sound of the Dremel, begin alternating these two pieces: tap with the Dremel, turn the Dremel on for two seconds, tap, Dremel sound, tap, Dremel sound. When the dog is familiar and accustomed to both, then and only then put them together. Don't worry about accomplishing anything with the first "live" Dremeling – just tap the toe, praise lavishly, and administered cheese.

Generously reward as you go, slowly progressing to more nails and more time on each nail. Do not stint on the food reinforcement: With enough Gouda, all things are possible.

Though it is tempting, do not acquiesce to your Ridgeback's reluctance to have his nails ground. Instead, proceed firmly but positively, even if you must do only one nail a night.

A Word About Bathing

Ridgebacks are wash-and-wear dogs – they typically don't need a lot of grooming. However, there will be times when your dog needs a bath. If you live in a warm climate, then a hose and a bottle of dog shampoo are all you need.

If you need to bathe your Ridgeback indoors, then you must get him accustomed to hopping in and out of a dog tub, bathtub or shower enclosure. But most Ridgebacks resist the idea of a bath. They are not Aquarians to begin with, and a bathtub or shower can seem claustrophobic. They also don't appreciate the slippery footing and lack of stability; adding a rubber mat to the floor of the tub is a must.

Using a Dremel rotary tool is the best way to trim Ridgeback nails. *Photo: ThruMarzenasLens.com*

As with all training involving Ridgebacks, the key is to start early and let him think it's his idea. As soon as the dog is old enough to see over the tub's edge, or walk into it, I build a positive association by feeding him treats in the tub. You can even serve his dinner in there. (Again, make sure the footing is not slippery and your puppy isn't panicking.)

As soon as he gets used to this and looks forward to being put in the tub, you can encourage him to put his feet up on the edge of the tub and give him a treat when he does. You might have to lure him into position with the treat, and if you do clicker training, this is a perfect application. I also like to leave treats in the tub at variable times and let him "discover" them on his own. This whole process builds an intensely positive association with the bathtub, and when it comes time to add water, your dog will likely handle it with little drama.

Again, when introducing water, don't just fill up the tub and plop him in. First turn the water on when he is outside the tub, and treat profusely. Then put him in the tub when there is only a half-inch or so of water present; again, lots of treats. When you feel he is ready, turn the water on for a few seconds when he is in the tub. Slowly, step by step, you'll turn him into a water lover yet.

Chapter 10

Nutrition

In human conversation, you're supposed to avoid discussing religion and politics. In dog circles, the subjects that are just as sure to start a disagreement are nutrition and vaccination.

In this chapter and the next, I'll discuss how I handle these two areas of dog care with my own dogs – and share what I suggest to my puppy people.

I want to stress that the opinions and suggestions here are my own, informed as they have been through decades of reporting and researching. I am not a veterinarian, and you should not use these chapters as a substitute for seeking treatment from a licensed veterinary professional.

The diets and vaccine protocols that I use may be very different from and even diametrically opposed to what your breeder suggests. While I think these methods are the optimal way to care for my dogs – otherwise I wouldn't be using them – I think that as a puppy owner, your first and best source of information is your breeder. No one knows *her* line of dogs better than she does.

You owe it to your breeder to inquire and then to listen – that second part is important – to what she has to say about how she'd like you to feed and vaccinate. In the end, you may opt to go in a different direction, but give your breeder the courtesy of hearing her opinions in full and understanding her position. Remember, your breeder is an expert on *her* dogs, and her insights are both hard earned and invaluable. Don't sell them short.

That said, many Ridgeback breeders are moving toward a more holistic approach to feeding their dogs. Concerned about autoimmune disease in the breed, many are seeking more natural and less invasive ways to rear them. That's what inspired me to start feeding a whole-food diet, and to really analyze just how many vaccines I was giving my dogs, and just how essential they were.

I realize that you may decide to feed dry dog food (kibble), or canned food, or a cooked, homemade diet. Those are all viable options that I've fed before, too. But this chapter is devoted to what I currently feed, which is a raw-food diet.

Raw Feeding

My philosophy of rearing dogs is pretty simple: Less is more, and the more natural and unprocessed, the better.

A lot of this may seem really obvious – and that's because it is. Feeding my dogs should not be more complicated than feeding my children. What do we know about optimal nutrition for humans? We know we should try to eat a varied diet, with as many whole, natural foods as possible, with as little processed food as possible. And to ensure that our bodies get the vitamins and minerals that they need, we take a multivitamin.

That is exactly how I feed my dogs.

Today, feeding raw isn't a radical, ground-breaking or – ubiquitous adjective for beginners – scary way to feed. There are even commercial brands of raw food, both frozen and dehydrated, available in mainstream pet stores.

But when I started feeding raw – a dozen years and four generations of Rhodesian Ridgebacks ago – it was the Middle Ages of raw feeding. Ian Billinghurst's "Feed Your Dog a Bone" book was the hard-to-find illuminated manuscript, and everyone used the unfortunate acronym BARF, which stood for "bones and raw food" (or, later, the loftier-sounding "biologically appropriate raw food"). No commercial raw diets were available, and new converts dutifully ordered their Maverick sausage grinders over the Internet. The instruction booklet said the table-top grinder couldn't be used on bones harder than chicken necks or wings, but everyone ignored that. I can still remember the painful whirring of the motor, and then the crackles and pops as the thin ropes of ground meat and bone came out the cylinder.

Think Holistically, Feed Locally

Like many people, I started feeding raw reactively, not proactively. I had a new dog, my first show dog and first Ridgeback, who just wasn't thriving on kibble. I remember setting down Blitz's first raw meal with great fear and trepidation. And then – anticlimax – he didn't choke, die or even look at me cross-eyed. He ate, he flourished, and off we went, and never looked back. Three more adult Ridgebacks followed, and dozens of puppies, who in turn had puppies of their own. All got their start in life on raw-food diets.

Back then (and still today), the Holy Grail of raw feeders was a quality meat source at affordable prices. Through local dog folk, I learned about Armellino's, a butcher in nearby Huntington Station, New York, who was a wholesaler of naturally reared poultry – chickens and turkeys raised without hormones or pesticides. Joe Armellino was your go-to guy for a free-range Thanksgiving dinner. And he had turkey necks – dare I hope? did I hear that right? – for less than a dollar a pound.

By my second or third trip there, as I gratefully accepted my 10-pound bag of turkey necks, Joe asked me quizzically, "Are you starting a soup business or something?"

"No," I replied with a chuckle. "I grind this stuff up for my dogs."

And as I explained the downsides of my feeding regimen – the noise, the blood, the guts, the time – lights started going off for Joe. Maybe he could buy a commercial grinder. Maybe he'd order that BARF book. This was a bit of back to the future: His father, from

Ridgeback puppies are weaned as early as three and a half to four weeks of age, but they'll never pass up a drink at the milk bar if at all possible. *Photo: Denise Flaim*

whom he had inherited the business, used to sell minced meat for dogs.

Today, many years later, my Ridgebacks still eat at Joe's. His business has gone to the dogs – literally – and his store walls are lined with dog photos, from Danes to Dachshunds, who get their sustenance there. Joe doesn't do mail order, he doesn't do any fancy packaging or marketing. He just gets the meat and bones directly from the source, grinds the whole lot, puts it in 2- or 5-pound sleeves, freezes it, and then sells it to the steady stream of doggie customers who are now a major part of his business.

Starting Off

My puppies are weaned on Joe's ground poultry mixed with evaporated milk at four weeks old. When the pups are around six weeks, I tell their new owners what I'm feeding, instruct them to order a good multivitamin and fish-oil source (for those nifty omega-3s), and have them stop by to visit Joe. (If they're not local, many will invest in a freezer and schlep back for a food run every few months.)

The three main problems with raw feeding for newbies are the time, the cost and the learning curve. Joe solves the first two: His food is convenient (just thaw out overnight, dump in the bowl, and add supplements) and affordable (about the same price as a high-quality kibble).

As for the learning curve, I've fed my family of dogs for multiple generations. I know what to expect in terms of their growth needs. The biggest advantage to feeding raw is being able to control what I feed. (Which is the disadvantage to commercially prepared raw diets, along with, frankly, price.) I am sure an Alaskan Malamute breeder instructs her puppy people to feed differently than I do, as would a Yorkie breeder.

"Half the pedigree goes through the mouth," the British say. You really are what you eat.

Red Light at the Vet's Office

Veterinarians are often the biggest obstacle to owners who would like to feed raw. And I understand why: They are worried about owners who will take shortcuts and compromise their dog's health in the process, far more than any fear of salmonella contamination. (After all, a pig's ear is crawling with the same bacteria.)

Any skeptical vet I have encountered has been put at ease when I tell him or her these two things: First, I know the source of my dog's meat, which is raised as holistically as anything I can buy in the supermarket for my own consumption; and second, I understand the importance of having a calcium source. The meat I feed has a more-than-adequate bone content, and it's finely ground to mitigate any issues of perforation or compaction. (Grinding the bones negates much of the teeth-cleaning benefit that comes from chomping on whole, uncooked bone, but life is nothing if not a series of compromises. And that's one I can live with.)

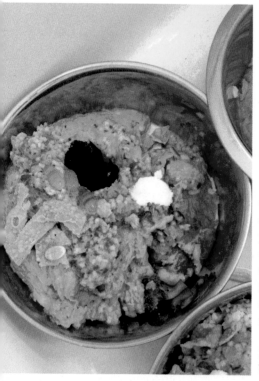

This meal includes raw ground chicken augmented with seaweed, coconut oil and Chinese-food leftovers.

"Well," the vet invariably says. "You've done your homework. But the average pet owner isn't as conscientious." Maybe so, but it's my job as a breeder to instruct my puppy people on how to feed correctly. And there's a huge piece of me that thinks the lowest common denominator is a terrible place at which to set the bar.

All this is not to say that raw-feeding is appropriate for every Ridgeback. It's not for dogs who are immune-compromised, or whose bodies are so depleted that they can't effectively deal with the everyday pathogens that a healthy dog would just shrug off. But I've seen dogs who have chronic environmental allergies react beautifully to a raw-food diet; ditto for dogs who were having anal-sac infections so severe that drastic surgery was being contemplated.

But curing a sick or ailing dog really shouldn't be your motivation for feeding a raw diet: It should be to keep your dog healthy in the first place.

Ridgebacks can get very pushy about food if you let them. *Photos: Denise Flaim*

In all the years I have been feeding this way, I haven't had any major health issues with my dogs. They stay vibrantly healthy and look like a million bucks. The longer I am in dogs, and the more I talk with old-time breeders who themselves are becoming an extinct breed, the more I take this simple truth to heart: No matter how fantastic a pedigree, it can be ruined by bad nutrition and bad rearing. Common sense prevails: Dogs need sunshine, exercise and good, whole, hydrated food.

Dog people – especially serious dog people – like to get all self-righteous about how they feed. It's our way or the highway. I want my puppies to be raw-fed and I strongly encourage that way of feeding (just as I do minimal vaccination and pesticide-free landscaping), but in the end I realize I don't have control. And I also realize that lifestyle and economics also impact how we care for our dogs. In an ideal world ... but who lives in an ideal world all their life?

My Ridgebacks aren't the only litters I have around the house: My human kids consist of 11-year-old triplets. When they were toddling, I was concerned about bacterial cross-contamination. And the cost of diapers and formula (I'm holistic, but breast-feeding triplets? – I'm not *that* holistic!) was beginning to make a real dent in our budget. So I began cooking the Armellino food, boiling it up in a pot with a grain source such as barley, to stretch it a little further. I did that for about two years, until the kids were bigger and could be trusted not to, say, lick the dogs' food bowls or stuff fistfuls of raw turkey in their mouths.

It wasn't until I looked back over that time that I noticed some subtle changes in my dogs. They were still generally healthy on the cooked, carb-loaded diet, but I noticed an increased frequency of acute problems: the occasional ear infection or impacted anal sac, for instance. A homeopathic vet suggested I start a journal to note these little changes, and if I had followed that advice during that period, I'm sure I would have noticed additional "nickle and dime" changes that the cooked food brought – and not for the better. If ever I needed proof of the price we pay when we destroy the enzymes and nutrients in our dogs' food by cooking it, there it was.

So, in my heart of hearts, do I think raw is better than home-cooked is better than canned is better than kibble is better than plasterboard? To be honest, yes. But do I think I loved my dogs any less by making the lifestyle and economic concessions that I needed to, when I needed to? To be honest, no.

In the end, what raw feeding taught me were the same life lessons we all take to heart: Never act out of a place of fear. Embrace common sense. (If whole foods are good for us, why should our dogs be any different?) Keep things simple. Act locally. (Thank you, Joe.) And master the use of the prepositional phrase "In my experience" at the beginning of any sentence involving a controversial subject like raw feeding. Because your experience is your experience, whether others agree or not.

The ABCs of Raw Feeding

If you are serious about feeding raw, do some research, and invest in a good book on the subject. Here are some tips to help you on your way:

• A raw-food diet does not mean that you can feed your Ridgeback raw hamburger meat and call it a day. At least 60 percent of what you are feeding *must* contain raw, uncooked bones. Without this bone source in his diet, your puppy will leach calcium from his own bones and develop orthopedic problems that are entirely avoidable.

• If possible, feed three times a day until your puppy is six months old. After six months, feed twice a day until your puppy reaches one year. You can switch to once a day at one year, or keep feeding twice daily for life.

• Keep a close eye on your puppy's weight and silhouette. As your puppy grows, increase the amount of food. I have found that some puppies need a carbohydrate source (such as rice or pasta) added to their diet during later puppyhood because their metabolism is so fast they literally cannot get enough nutrients from a raw-only diet.

• The more variety of meat you can provide, the better. I use my butcher's poultry mix as a base because it is the most reasonably priced, and the dogs seem to do best on it. But I also add extras, including any leftovers from the humans in the household (excluding, of course, problematic vegetables such as raw onions, as well as cooked bones).

• To make sure your dog gets all the nutrition she needs, feed a multi-vitamin daily. You can use a human brand, such as One a Day. Use an appropriate-size vitamin or a portion of a vitamin that corresponds to your puppy's weight. You will have to crush the vitamin

Try to keep your Ridgeback's lifestyle as chemical-free as possible. Diet is a big part of that. *Photo: Rickardo Curenton*

into a powder until your puppy is old enough to swallow the pill whole.

• I supplement with fish body oil (which is *not* the same as cod-liver oil!). Fish oil provides omega-3 fatty acids, which act as anti-inflammatories in the body and bolster the immune system. Be sure the oil you are feeding is high quality, as impurities and toxins such as mercury are a concern with any ocean fish. Until your puppy is big enough to swallow the gel cap, stick a pin in it and squeeze the contents onto the food.

• Pay special attention to calcium intake, especially until your puppy reaches seven to eight months of age. In addition to feeding whole milk, I also add a hard-boiled egg, shell and all. The signs of inadequate calcium levels include flat feet and "flying nun ears," which cannot be reversed once the puppy reaches a certain age.

• Raw-fed Ridgeback will be lean and will grow slowly and consistently. They have less of an odor than kibble-fed dogs, and will be less likely to get allergies or ear infections, a common problem in the breed.

A raw-fed dog's stool has much less volume than that of a kibble-fed dog – about a third – and it will not smell as foul, because it contains no preservatives. If you forget to scoop it, after a week or so it just turns white and crumbles. Poof!

• As with anything in life, there are safeguards to consider. Bacteria in raw meat does exist, but most healthy canine digestive systems are well equipped to handle things like salmonella and E coli. Human digestive tracts, however, are not, so it is important that you observe proper hygiene and wash your hands and your work area, just as you would if preparing raw meat for yourself. Be sure to clean the dog's bowl with hot, soapy water after each feeding.

• If you have immunocompromised humans in the household, or very young children, you can simply cook the meat, if the bones are ground in. Alternately, some proponents of home-cooking use a slow-cooker, which cooks the bones to the point where they essentially disintegrate. Never feed cooked whole bones, as the risk of impaction or perforation is simply too high.

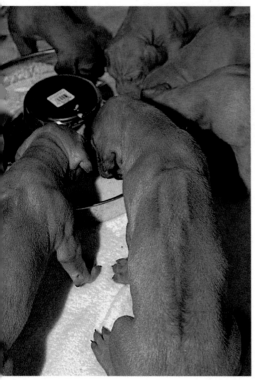

Soup's on! *Photo: Jens Ratsey-Woodroffe*

The biggest risk to feeding raw is "migrating" off the diet and not providing the proper bone content.

• To gauge whether you are feeding the right amount of food, just use common sense: If your dog looks too thin, feed him more; if he looks too chubby, cut down on the amount you are giving him. Rule of thumb: The average raw-fed dog consumes about 2 percent of his body weight in meat daily.

Don't Panic

If you've opted to feed your dog a raw-food diet, it's important to remember that a lot of the so-called "norms" for dogs are based on data on kibble-fed dogs. As a result, your mileage can and often will vary.

For example, a 2003 study done by Dr. Jean Dodds in collaboration with Dr. Susan Wynn found that dogs fed raw meat had higher red blood cell and blood urea nitrogen, or BUN, levels than dogs fed cereal-based food. High BUN levels will usually set off the alarm bells at your vet's office, because they can signal compromised kidney function.

Don't assume that your vet knows that higher BUN levels are normal in raw-fed dogs: Several years ago, a puppy person of mine took her dog to be spayed; when Dakota's pre-surgical bloodwork showed an elevated BUN level, a newbie veterinarian at the practice admitted the dog and put her on fluids. The worried owner called me, and I in turn called the senior vet, who then pulled the plug on the unnecessary treatment.

"Are you going to finish that?" Ridgebacks have no shame when it comes to food.
Photo: Dreamstime

Another area of undue concern with raw-fed dogs is water consumption. If you are accustomed to living with kibble-fed dogs, a raw-feeder will appear to be a camel by comparison. That's because unlike kibble, which has its moisture content extracted in order to increase its shelf life, raw meat is very well hydrated: Raw-fed dogs aren't constantly slurping up water because it hasn't been removed from their food to begin with. I can't tell you how many puppy people have called me over the years, seriously concerned because their new puppy has only taken a cursory sip of water. If the puppy is behaving and playing normally, I tell them, don't worry.

Of course, there are diseases that can cause a dog to lower her water intake, and any significant change in water consumption should be cause for concern. And you should always have fresh water available, no matter what your dog's diet comprises.

Fat or Fit?

The recipe for an overweight Ridgeback contains just one ingredient:

Opportunity.

Though there are exceptions, Ridgebacks are notorious chowhounds. With cast-iron stomachs and insatiable appetites, they will eat with all the fervor of a contestant at a hot-dog-eating competition – if you let them.

Do not free-feed! Veterinarians who encourage their clients to feed their puppies "all they can eat for 15 minutes" clearly have little to no experience with this breed. Most Ridgebacks will eat as long as there is food in front of them. If you have served your dog an adequate portion and he still seems dissatisfied, you can "bulk" up his next meal with filling but low-calorie additions such as green beans or canned pumpkin (not pumpkin-pie mix, which has sugar and spices).

Ravenous does not equal starved. Most Ridgebacks always seem hungry. Just because yours acts as if he has not eaten in a week doesn't mean you should feed him if he has already had adequate nutrition for the day. Don't fall for the guilt trip!

A trim Ridgeback is a healthy Ridgeback. Keeping extra weight off your dog will not only make her look and feel good, but it will also help prevent injury. Ridgebacks are by nature athletic and enthusiastic dogs, and they can easily hurt themselves if their excessive body weight impairs their agility.

That goes double for puppies! A roly-poly puppy may be cute, but that extra weight puts a strain on growing bones and connective tissue, and could provoke orthopedic problems. Lean, svelte puppies are best.

Rule out an underlying medical cause. Hypothyroidism, which is not uncommon in Ridgebacks, can cause dramatic weight gain. If your Ridgeback is putting on pounds despite a reasonable diet, have your vet perform a simple blood test to check your dog's thyroid levels. If your dog turns out to have an underactive thyroid, twice-daily medication will return his metabolism back to normal – and with it, his body weight.

Discourage countersurfing. If you leave food items unattended on tables and countertops, your Ridgeback will learn to jump up and help herself. This happens with a stealth that is equally impressive and infuriating. Be diligent about putting away tempting foods in places where they cannot be swiped, or you will encourage a habit that is notoriously hard to break. (Microwaves are a great hiding spot.)

Seek out an experienced eye. Unfortunately, many veterinarians are not familiar with correct Ridgeback weight and conditioning, and may actually think an overweight Ridgeback is "normal." If you obtained your dog from a reputable breeder or a Ridgeback rescue group, that's the best place to ask, "Is she too fat?" (This can be as simple as emailing a few photographs – one taken from the side, one taken from above. Make sure

At left, two views of the same female Ridgeback: At top, at a normal and correct weight; below, severely overweight. Study these comparisons carefully, because to the uninitiated, there many not appear to be much difference between the two. When they gain weight, Ridgebacks tend to simply "blow up," like a balloon, so they don't develop bulges or muffin tops – they just expand proportionately. But the bottom dog is at least 15 pounds heavier; she looks "matronly," even though she has never had puppies. Telltale signs are her thick, heavy neck, and an overall fullness to her form. Notice that her belly is also hanging below her tuck-up compared to the first photo. Not visible here is the "dimple" of fat above the tail.

Above: Another obese Ridgeback. Note the thick neck, wide girth and folds of fat on her back. Below: Side-by-side comparison of an overweight Ridgeback (left) and a normally sized one. Note the telltale fat "dimple" above the overweight dog's tail. *Photos: Fred Eder*

the dog is standing.) If you don't have those resources, go to a local dog show and observe the Ridgebacks being exhibited.

Ridgebacks can vary considerably in size, and many weigh slightly more than the guidelines listed in the official standard (85 pounds for males and 70 pounds for females). However, a male that weighs more than 100 pounds, and a female that clocks in at over 80 pounds, is likely overweight.

If you do not spend time around well-conditioned Ridgebacks who are in good weight, it can be hard to know just what your Ridgeback should look like. He should not have the beefy outline of a Labrador retriever, but rather, a trim, athletic silhouette that suggests a dog that can run all day and never tire.

Your first hint is the underline. Looking at your Ridgeback from the side, the bottom of the chest should not be a straight parallel line all the way to his rear legs. Instead, he should have a clearly defined tuckup that follows the tapering of his ribs up to his loin. If you can't see this "waist," your Ridgeback is likely overweight.

Second, consider the "aerial view." Look down at your Ridgeback and follow his ribcage to the end. On a fit and trim Ridgeback, there should be a natural indentation and narrowing where the ribs end and the loin begins, just before the legs. On an overweight Ridgeback, this just looks like a straight line (or a bulging one!).

Finally, an overweight Ridgeback will have a beefy, stocky look. There might be rolls around his neck and dimpling

Need a reference point? Go to a dog show. The Ridgebacks there will likely be at an appropriate weight, as this one is. *Photo: Theresa M. Lyons*

on his hindquarters just above his tail. This is not muscle – it's fat!

You owe it to your Ridgeback to make sure that she is in fit condition. Being fat is not an emblem of how much you love your dog – it's simply an unnecessary health risk.

Loss of appetite? Warning bells. Ridgebacks are notorious chowhounds – they'll eat whatever is not nailed down. If your Ridgeback is off his food, it is a cause for concern. Monitor the situation closely and, if the lack of appetite persists, seriously consider a visit to the vet. A Ridgeback that does not eat is often a very sick Ridgeback.

Games at mealtime. Ridgebacks are very smart; if they can find a way to manipulate you to give them better food instead of the regular meal that you're serving, they'll give it the good old college try. It's up to you to be smarter than they are.

Occasionally, puppies will inexplicably lose interest in their food. If this is the case, and your Ridgeback is normal in all other ways – play levels, normal stools, overall energy and vitality – you may have a picky eater in the making. This is rare but not unheard of in Ridgebacks. The solution with a picky eater is to ignore her. Do not sit legs akimbo on the floor with the bowl in your lap, begging your baby to eat her dinner. Present the food matter-of-factly, give her a few minutes to eat it, and if she does not, scoop it up, put it in the fridge and wait till the next mealtime.

Chapter 11

Vaccination and Spay/Neuter

Never mind puppy breath: What a new puppy really reeks of is possibility. Every new experience and interaction helps nudge your recent arrival toward the dog he will one day become.

And the same applies to his health care and rearing: How you vaccinate, when your vet performs certain procedures, the environment you place him in – all will contribute to his future health and vibrancy.

Vaccination

Vaccinating your Ridgeback is a bit of a seesaw act: On the one hand, you don't want to overtax her immune system with unnecessary vaccines; on the other, you want to make sure she is protected against serious diseases that can threaten her life.

As with that piece of playground equipment, the answer is *balance*.

After decades of reflexively vaccinating the family dog with "annual shots," veterinary medicine is now acknowledging that, when it comes to vaccination, less is oftentimes more. Some veterinarians argue that overvaccination opens the door to autoimmune disease, such as hemolytic anemia, allergies and cancer, all of which occur in Ridgebacks, the latter two with more frequency. Others dispute this – hotly – by saying there is no direct proof of case and effect. But what most everyone agrees on is that vaccination is a medical procedure that should be weighed carefully by owner and vet alike.

Some puppy owners go so far as to not vaccinate at all. But the vast majority do some form of vaccination, and that is where I land. The question is: What vaccines and how often?

A middle ground that many progressive breeders follow are the canine vaccination guidelines offered by the American Animal Hospital Association, or AAHA. (Say that cheekily: "AH-ha!")

AAHA divides vaccines into three categories: "core," or must have; "non-core," which might be appropriate, depending on your dog's risk factors; and the flat-out "not recommended."

AAHA lists only four vaccines as "core": parvovirus, distemper and adenovirus (also known as canine hepatitis), which are given as part of the puppy series starting as early as six weeks; and rabies, which is initially given at three months or later.

If you want to follow the AAHA protocol, don't assume that your vet can automatically accommodate you: Not all vets carry the trivalent, or 3-in-1, vaccine for parvo, distemper

NON-CORE	NOT RECOMMENDED
Canine Parainfluenza	Canine Coronavirus
Canine Influenza Virus	Canine Adenovirus 1 (CAD-1)
Distemper-Measles Combo	Rattlesnake envenomation
Bordetella	
Leptospirosis	
Lyme	

and adenovirus. Instead, your vet may only stock 5-in-1 or even 7-in-1 vaccines (which contain non-core vaccines such as parainfluenza and, in the case of the latter, even non-recommended ones such as coronavirus, which is not a risk for puppies older than six weeks). If you call in advance, your vet will have time to order the 3-in-1 vaccine – or you will have time to find another practice that has it on hand.

As for the vaccines that AAHA lists as non-core, think about whether these optional vaccines make sense in the context of your dog's lifestyle. If your dog never goes to boarding facilities or dog runs, does it make sense to vaccinate for bordetella (commonly known as kennel cough)? If you live in a part of the country where ticks are relatively uncommon, is it necessary to give the Lyme vaccine?

Another area of disagreement is how frequently vaccines should be given. Some veterinary immunologists point to evidence that shows immunity to the core vaccines can last as long as five to seven years. The middle-of-the-road AAHA protocol recommends revaccinating no more frequently than every three years for parvo, distemper or adenovirus.

Because it is mandated by state law, rabies, however, is non-negotiable. Most states require a three-year interval, though a handful still stipulate revaccination annually.

If all this sounds like a lot of work, that's because it is. In order for you to help your vet arrive at a minimal but safe vaccination schedule for your puppy, you need to educate yourself about individual vaccines and their relative risks and benefits.

A Suggested Vaccine Protocol

The vaccine schedule I use for my Ridgeback puppies is a modified version of the schedule suggested by Dr. W. Jean Dodds, a well-respected veterinarian and immunologist. She advocates vaccinating for the three major threats – distemper, parvovirus and rabies – and does not recommend vaccinating for Bordetella, coronavirus, leptospirosis or Lyme unless those diseases are endemic in the area where the dog lives.

Though AAHA considers it a core vaccine, adenovirus is not included in Dr. Dodds' protocol, as is a mild respiratory infection, and the other disease that this vaccine protects against, canine hepatitis, is a rarity. In fact, it is likely that your vet has never encountered a case of canine hepatitis in the last two decades, if at all.

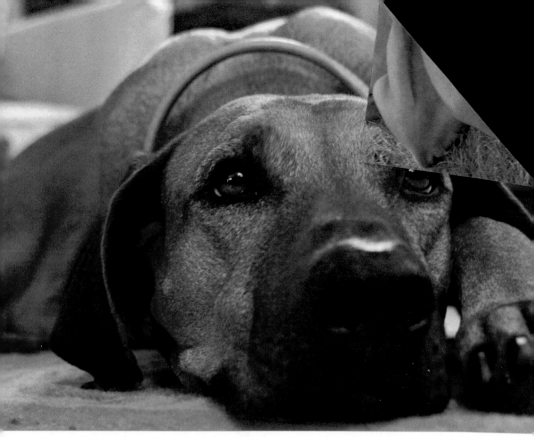

Once your Ridgeback reaches adulthood, she does not require annual "boosters." You can check her immunity levels with a blood test called a titer. *Photo: ThruMarzenasLens.com*

DR. JEAN DODDS CANINE VACCINATION PROTOCOL	
Age	**Vaccine Recommendation**
9-10 weeks old	Distemper + Parvovirus, MLV (e.g. Merck Nobivac [Intervet Progard] Puppy DPV)
14-16 weeks old	Same as above
20 Weeks or older (if allowable by law)	Rabies
1 Year	Distemper + Parvovirus, MLV (optional = titer)
1 Year after initial dose	Rabies, killed 3-year product (give 3-4 weeks apart from distemper/parvovirus booster)
	Perform vaccine antibody titers for distemper and parvovirus every three years thereafter, or more often, if desired. Vaccinate for rabies virus according to the law, except where circumstances indicate that a written waiver needs to be obtained from the primary care veterinarian. In that case, a rabies antibody titer can also be performed to accompany the waiver request.

Puppies should be vaccinated against diseases that kill – among them parvovirus, distemper and rabies.

Though canine hepatitis is believed to have been eradicated in the American domestic dog population, pockets of infection cropped up in California a decade ago, brought across the border by Mexican dogs. And a recent case of canine-hepatitis infection in New Hampshire that took the lives of two Ridgeback puppies was believed to have been transmitted by a Canadian red fox.

Why not just vaccinate for canine hepatitis, then? Because when that vaccine is administered at the same time as the distemper vaccine, and both vaccine viruses replicate in the body simultaneously, immunosuppression can occur. This hiccup of the immune system starts about three days after vaccination and can continue for up to 10 days. For that week-long span, the puppy is immunologically vulnerable, with a compromised immune system.

My solution to this dilemma is to vaccinate my puppies the first time with a parvovirus-distemper vaccine only. When the puppies are due for their second vaccination a month later, I instruct the owners to do the three-way vaccine, with adenovirus included. I also make another modification to Dr. Dodds' protocol: Because I don't want to send puppies to their new homes unvaccinated, I do their first vaccinations a bit early, at 7½ or 8 weeks old.

Administering Vaccines

Even if your veterinarian administers only one "shot," there could be multiple vaccines in that syringe. Find out what your dog is getting before that cap comes off the needle.

Always vaccinate for rabies separately. This goes for other "killed" vaccines, such as leptospirosis, too. The adjuvants, or preservatives, used in these types of vaccines can cause adverse vaccine reactions. So, in order not to overload your dog's immune system, schedule a few weeks between "booster" shots and these killed vaccines.

Remind your vet not to administer the vaccine anywhere on your Ridgeback's dorsal midline. As I mentioned earlier, you do not want any injection-site swelling to be confused with a dermoid sinus.

You are the ultimate arbiter of your dog's health. Make your decisions intelligently, with adequate research and understanding – not just because "the vet said so."

Spaying and Neutering

As a Ridgeback breeder, I screen my homes carefully. I have legalese-dotted contracts that require any dog of my breeding to be returned to me if he is no longer wanted, regardless of reason or age or health condition. And, of course, I require that all puppies that I sell as companions be spayed and neutered.

But in recent years, my attitude on that last score has begun to evolve, in large part due to new health information that has come to the fore. My contracts still require those lovely and loved companions to be altered, and in more than a decade I have never had any reproduce (at least as far as I know!). But the parameters of when I want spay/neuter surgeries done have changed, and likely will continue to.

While no one questions the importance of spay/neuter as a tool to stem animal overpopulation, the questions on the table are: Does one size fit all? Should committed, responsible people review the facts and scientific literature to make an individualized decision for their particular dog? What are the real risks of keeping a dog intact for some period of time, balanced against a growing body of evidence showing that early spay/neuter might be implicated in a number of orthopedic, oncological and even behavioral problems?

Before we talk about spay/neuter in pragmatic terms – what the studies say, what the different scenarios are – we need to acknowledge its emotional charge. If you doubt this, walk an unneutered male on the street in any major city in America, and count how many looks of revulsion and unsolicited verbal reproaches you generate.

The cultural message is clear: Responsible people spay and neuter their companion animals. Those who don't are derelict in their civic duty.

This is in sharp contrast to attitudes elsewhere in the world, particularly in many parts of Europe, where unaltered dogs are common. In Norway, it is illegal to spay or neuter a dog without a valid medical reason. The rationale is that it is morally wrong to surgically alter a dog for human whim or convenience, which puts spay/neuter on a par with ear cropping and tail docking. But reportedly everything is not rosy when spay/neuter is severely curtailed, either: One news article I read mentioned increased rates of pyometra, which is a potentially life-threatening uterine infection, and injuries from dogs scrapping it up.

For many years, proponents of early spay/neuter have argued its health benefits: In females, some studies have shown that spaying before the first heat cycle virtually eliminates the risk of mammary cancer, though more recent analysis has cast doubt on the methodologies and validities of many of them. And everyone is in agreement that spaying prevents pyometra, which is serious and potentially fatal.

In males, neutering removes the possibility of testicular cancer as well as reduces the risk of prostate enlargement and infection later in life. And in both sexes, spay/neuter is believed to eliminate unwanted behaviors, in particular aggression toward other dogs and people.

In recent years, some veterinarians who have been concerned about the risks of early spay-neuter have begun to catalog its drawbacks. One is abnormal growth – such as longer limbs, lighter bone structure, and narrow chests and skulls – in dogs altered at a young age because the absence of testosterone delays the closing of the growth plates. This isn't just a cosmetic concern: The lengthening of the long bones creates a significantly higher risk of osteosarcoma, or bone cancer, in dogs altered at younger than one year.

Included on the list of problems associated with early spay/neuter are greater risk of hemangiosarcoma, mast cell cancer, lymphoma and bladder cancer; higher incidence of hip dysplasia in dogs spayed or neutered at six months of age; significantly higher prevalence of cranial cruciate ligament (CCL) injury; heightened risk of urinary incontinence in females that are spayed early, as well as some cases in males; greater likelihood of hypothyroidism in spayed and neutered dogs; higher incidence of infectious diseases in dogs spayed and neutered at 24 weeks or less; higher incidence of adverse reactions to vaccines in altered dogs; and increased risk of prostate cancer in neutered males.

Does it make sense to think that you can remove a puppy's major reproductive organs – and all the hormones that go with it – and not expect there to be some biological ramifications?

To be sure, there are health risks in keeping a dog, especially a female, intact. Personally, unless a female is being used for breeding, I can't find a justification for keeping her unspayed indefinitely. For me, it's a question of not *if* to spay, but *when* to.

The two biggest health benefits cited for spaying females before their first heat are reduced risk of mammary cancer – which some experts dispute – and the elimination of pyometra, which is an unambiguous and valid concern: Studies show that almost a quarter of intact females will experience this infection of the uterus by the time they are 10 years old.

In terms of my own puppy owners, I have encourage them to allow their female puppies to go through one heat cycle before spaying – provided they know what they are getting into and can house her securely for that three-week period. Though there are no studies to confirm this, anecdotal evidence suggests that allowing the body to go through a heat allows the genitalia to mature normally, avoiding or resolving inverted vulvas that can lead to incontinence. It also permits the maturation of estrogen receptors, which might also play a role in incontinence, a known risk of spay surgery.

The oft-quoted 1969 study about the correlation between spaying and mammary cancer says that females spayed before their first heat have almost a zero chance of developing mammary cancer; after the first heat, that risk rises to 8 percent, and 26 percent after the second. Beyond that point, the study says, the protective aspect of spaying is negligible. Even before that study was called into question, I always thought that an 8 percent increased risk of mammary cancer was a chance was worth taking, if allowing the dog to mature sexually helped protect against other cancers and various orthopedic concerns. Mammary cancer isn't the only thing female dogs can die from – it is one concern among many.

Since our experience colors things, my attitude also likely has to do with the fact that I have not had much experience with mammary cancer being a problem in my intact females or those of fellow breeders. That is not to say that it won't happen – and as soon as you say, "Not me!" it usually does – but for the moment, cancers like lymphoma and hemangiosarcoma are anecdotally more prevalent, even among the retired breeding bitches I know.

In many respects, thinking outside the box about delaying neutering in males is a little easier: The health ramifications, while still there, are not as dire as for females.

Testicular cancer is still a concern, but is easily detectable. A bigger problem, I've found, is prostatitis in intact males, especially older ones that are sexually stimulated by intact females in the household. If a prostate infection develops, and leads to an abscess, it can be difficult to diagnose. I almost lost an unneutered older male to an abscess that had thankfully not yet gone into sepsis –but I have had friends who were not as lucky.

Some owners of intact males complain about marking behavior, though I've never had that be an issue, unless it's with a new intact male who comes to visit. Once he settles in and gets used to the girl scent, he gets over his temptation to lift a leg, and a vigilant eye and a belly band (that cummerbund-styled "diaper") have always done the trick for me until he does.

Because of health considerations, my puppy contracts currently ask that male puppies not be neutered before 12 month, ideally 18 months. Some people are willing to wait, most aren't, and that's OK: I tell them to hang on for as long as they can. But if their male dog

Prostate infection is a concern in older, unneutered males. *Photo: Dreamstime*

is going to visit a dog park on a regular basis, then I tell them to neuter before he really begins to elicit a response from the neutered adult males there – usually by 10 months of age. If not, one day when his hormonal signature becomes a threat, the neutered dogs will go for him (though he will be blamed, because he is the intact one), and his happy-go-lucky attitude toward other dogs will change forever. And that's just not worth an extra couple of months of testosterone in my book.

Among my fellow breeders, the idea of delaying spay/neuter is no longer a hot button. Not everyone advocates it, but pretty much everyone respects your right to take a different approach – as long as all the people involved are responsible.

The bottom line is that it is important to make an informed choice based on knowledge, not emotion. And once that choice is made – no matter what choice it is – realize there are consequences.

Chapter 12

Don't Panic!

If you live with and love Ridgebacks, chances are at some point you'll find yourself at an often excruciating tipping point.

"I just noticed (fill-in-the-blank)," you'll say to yourself. "Should I panic?"

The standard response that everyone gives – and for good reason – is: When in doubt, see your vet. And, of course, you should, if you suspect something is truly amiss. But you can't go running to a medical professional every time you notice something weird, especially if it's more an issue of benign bemusement rather than an out-and-out emergency. Problem is, you don't know what you don't know: Something that may seem really strange could be absolutely nothing, and a seemingly subtle symptom could be a harbinger of something truly disastrous.

Folks who have been "in Ridgebacks" for a good length of time often amass a tremendous storehouse of practically gained knowledge: After all, familiarity breeds knowledge as much as contempt, and when it comes to your dog, that can come in very handy. And oftentimes, "Ridgeback people" are willing to share advice with novices, if only to help them sift out the trivialities from the true alarm bells. For this reason, your breeder will be an invaluable sounding board for anything that concerns you.

I've been on the receiving end of panicked phone calls for a number of years, and on occasion I still make them, too. Here are some of the "emergencies" that turned out, happily, to be nothing to worry about. Again, reading about my personal experiences is no substitute for veterinary care, but at the very least you can add it to your storehouse of knowledge. Somewhere down the line, you might just need it.

As always, be sure to consult a qualified veterinary medical professional if you have the slightest concern about your dog's health and well-being.

Here's Looking at You – or Not

The third eyelid, sometimes colloquially called the haw, is a translucent, milky-white membrane that is usually not visible in dogs. Sometimes an eye injury, such as a scratched cornea, will cause the third eyelid to cover the eye, in order to protect it; some ophthalmological conditions, such as cherry eye (which is rare in Ridgebacks), can also cause the haw to be visible and prominent. In those situations, a veterinary consult is needed and necessary.

But more typically, you'll notice the third eyelid when your dog is dozing, in that middle ground between asleep and awake, when her eyes are darting around in dream mode and

Above left: Worry not! During sleep, the nictitating membrane, or "third eyelid," may be visible. Above right: A Ridgeback with a corneal scratch; in injuries such as these, the membrane partially covers the eye for protection. In this case, see a vet!

her eyelids are partially open. It looks a little freaky, but once she stops her slumber, the membrane will slip back where it belongs – out of sight. Rather than calling the Vatican for an exorcism, just know that this is normal and there's absolutely nothing to be concerned about.

Bug Bites

Like any dog, Ridgebacks shouldn't live under glass, and there will be times when yours is outdoors and encounters a creepy-crawly. Stings and bites from bees and spiders can cause your Ridgeback to have an allergic reaction. Sometimes the face swells so that badly your dog could be mistaken for a hippopotamus, or at least a Sharpei. Other times her body might become covered with hives. If the reaction is severe, by all means get your dog to the veterinarian. If there is time, or if there is no veterinarian available, be sure to administer Benadryl – 1 mg per pound of body weight is the rule of thumb. This should help to bring the inflammation down. In most cases after a few hours or longer your dog will gradually return to normal. The concern with this, as with any kind of allergic reaction, is that the dog's airways will close and impede breathing, which could be life-threatening. Monitor your dog carefully, and, when in doubt, head to the vet.

"Grass Bumps"

There's probably a technical name for these lozenge-shaped bumps that sometimes appear on the top of the head, neck and flanks, but I don't know it. What I do know is that these can be very perplexing to new Ridgeback owners, who naturally think they are caused by insect bites. But these bumps are much longer lasting (sometimes lingering for days), do not seem to be affected by antihistamines such as Benadryl, and are not accompanied by facial swelling or other signs of inflammation. The only thing that I have found that brings them down is the application of a towel that is saturated with water, rung out, put in the freezer until it is almost frozen, and then draped over the affected areas.

As their informal name suggests, "grass bumps" tend to appear after a Ridgeback has had contact with the sap of certain vegetation. Traversing a newly mown lawn can often bring them on; I've also seen a puppy chomping on a newly green hydrangea bush quickly become covered with them.

I tend to see these bumps in younger dogs, and by the time they reach adulthood, most have outgrown this reaction. The way to avoid them is to keep the dog off freshly mown lawns, or to wipe the pads of her feet with a clean, wet cloth after she has been on one.

Top: A puppy with a vaccine reaction. Bottom: Viral papilloma on an adolescent Ridgeback.

"Growth Warts"

You look under your puppy's chin, and, horror of horrors, it looks like some alien creature has taken over: Bumpy, pustule-like growths that resemble mini-cauliflowers cover the bottom of the jaw, and in some cases may even spread onto the lips and inside the mouth.

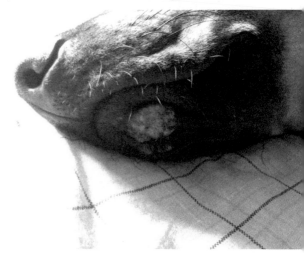

In all likelihood, what you're seeing is viral papilloma. Like most viruses, it won't respond to antibiotics, and – as with many things – the best treatment is tincture of time. Eventually the virus will run its course. What you can do in the meantime is keep your puppy's immune system vibrant and healthy so he can fight the virus.

Very severe cases – which can spread to the area around the eyes and even toes – might require veterinary intervention, although effective treatment is elusive. A holistic vet can prescribe homeopathic remedies that might shorten the duration of the virus.

Suddenly surfacing "dermoids"

Experienced Ridgebacks owners are very careful about the location of any vaccines given

to their puppies. The reason is that any lump or bump on the midline, especially on a young puppy, can be mistaken for a dermoid sinus. In the early years of the breed, there are accounts of breeders who euthanized puppies because they found "dermoids" that suddenly surfaced at eight weeks of age. Sadly, what they were seeing were injection-site reactions.

Weird Coat Pattern #1

If you're like most people, once you got interested in the breed, you scoured the Internet looking at endless streams of Ridgeback photos, and tried to meet as many as possible. So you've seen the breed.

But have you really *looked* at it? Because if you did, you'd have noticed that there are lighter-colored areas of fur near the top portion of the shoulder, and along the "britches," or back of the rear thighs. Someone came up with the charming name "angel wings," but whatever you call them, these areas of lighter coat color are simply a natural patterning, and have always been there. Chances are you just never noticed.

Weird Coat Pattern #2

Depending on the time of year, Ridgebacks can and do molt. When they are "blowing coat," they can look like miniature yaks, with tufts of fluffy undercoat wafting in the breeze. This tendency seems to be dependent on individual lines, and many dogs with short, slick coats will never undergo this metamorphosis. But if yours does, know that your Cinderella awaits under all that pouf.

Weird Coat Pattern #3

Another issue you might see with your Ridgeback's coat is seasonal flank alopecia.

Above: "Angel wings," the light area visible below and to the right of the top of the ridge. Below: a classic example of seasonal flank alopecia.

Those three words say it all: "Seasonal," meaning it often coincides with the changing of the seasons (typically between November and March in North America); "flank," referring to the sides of the dog, which are what is affected; and "alopecia," a fancy way of saying hair loss.

Other conditions can cause similar hair loss, including demodectic mange, ringworm infection, hypothyroidism and Cushing's disease, so be sure to rule those out.

These bald areas often become darkened with exposure, and can look really unattractive, though they are not painful to the dog and are a purely cosmetic problem. They are thought to be associated with light-related interruptions of hormone production, which in turn affect the hair follicles.

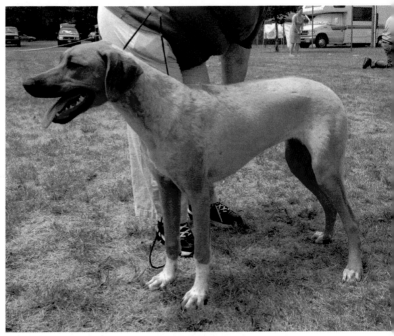

A Ridgeback undergoing a very dramatic "molt." Her coat later came in the same color as her head and legs.

Some Ridgeback owners have had success with melatonin supplementation. Also, because seasonal flank alopecia is the doggie version of seasonal affective disorder in humans, consider increasing direct exposure to sunlight or replacing fluorescent or incandescent bulbs with full-spectrum lighting, readily available at most hardware and home-improvement stores.

"Traveling" Limp

Orthopedic problems are always a worry in young dogs, especially in larger breeds. I've had more than one dog inexplicably come up lame between the ages of six to 18 months, visibly limping on one leg or unable to put weight on it. Often the limp "travels" from one limb to another, and always gets worse with exercise. It looks pretty dramatic, and it's easy to assume that it's something very serious.

In all those cases, though, what I was dealing with was paneosteitis – a fancy word for "growing pains." No one knows what causes it, though there are plenty of theories, from high-protein dog food to viral infection to genetics. What everyone agrees on is that while pano is painful, eventually the dog outgrows the condition, and returns to normal.

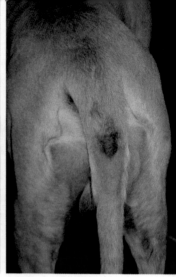

Top left: Grass eating can cause dogs to vomit bile. Top right: "Stud dog tail" on a Mastiff. *Photo: Dreamstime*

Paneosteitis is common in a number of breeds, including Rottweilers, Great Danes, German Shepherds and, yes, Rhodesian Ridgebacks. When a puppy owner of mine reports that telltale "traveling" limp, I usually suggest administering a baby aspirin (never, ever ibuprofen products like Advil, which are toxic to dogs). If it is pano, the aspirin will usually relieve the pain within an hour or so (though it will likely return once the drug wears off). There is no treatment for pano other than that old standby, tincture of time; keep the dog from being too active (good luck with that!) and consult your veterinarian about pain meds if the discomfort appears too great.

It's helpful if you know if pano runs in your dog's lines. Again, don't assume that your vet will suspect pano, even if your dog is the "right" age and breed for it. (Google "pano" and "Basset Hound," and you'll find plenty of links where veterinarians suspected – and in some cases, tested and even treated for – everything from elbow dysplasia to cancer.) X-rays will reveal changes in the bone marrow that are indicative of paneosteitis.

"Stud-Dog Tail"

Some Rigebacks have a triangle of black fur on their tails, about a third of the way down. This often disappears in adulthood, though sometimes a trace remains.

This black hair also marks the location of the supracaudal gland, which is a sebaceous scent gland present in wild canids such as foxes, domestic cats and some dog breeds, including Ridgebacks. Sometimes, when too much of the male sex hormone androgen is produced, the gland becomes overactive ("tail gland hyperplasia"), and there is hair loss over the area. Often, the skin will become crusty and scaly.

Though its name reflects the fact that it is more common among intact males, "stud dog tail" can appear in females and unneutered males, too. Unless the gland is infected, many vets opt to leave it alone; some will suggest neutering. Home remedies include cleaning the area with shampoo to clear the pores; some cat owners report success with lightly rubbing a paste made of sugar and water into the area, letting it sit and then rinsing out.

The Birds and the Bees

I promise I am not making this up: I had one puppy person, a very nice lady, email me in a panic about the severe flea bites on her puppy's belly. A picture is worth a thousand words, and once I reviewed the one she sent me, I responded and told her she could relax: Those weren't flea bites. They were nipples.

You can laugh, but with the prevalence of spaying and neutering, we have lost touch with our sense of animals as sexual beings. Since the dogs don't use those "parts," many owners have no idea what is normal or not regarding them.

News flash: Male dogs have nipples, just like male humans do, though they are not immediately visible, even on short-haired dogs like Ridgebacks. Unlike male humans, who have only two, boy dogs have multiple pairs. And theirs don't work, either.

Speaking of male dogs, you should know that neutering usually but doesn't always eliminate their ability to achieve what we'll delicately call a state of readiness. Owners who are distraught to see what they think is a penile infection might in fact be seeing the prelude to an erection: If you see a protruding something that resembles a pink lipstick cylinder, that's basically your signal that Buster is very, er, happy.

Snippety Snip

Everybody knows that male dogs are neutered in order to prevent them from procreating, but a surprising number of people don't know that this process involves removing the testicles. After bringing their dog home after the procedure, some owners grow concerned that those dangly bits were never removed, since it appears that they've reappeared. The reality: Post-surgical blood pooling in the scrotum, which is not removed, can make it seem as if the dog still has his "boys." Keep an eye out for infection or a break in the wound, and, of course, call your vet if you are concerned.

Not-So-Mellow Yellow

The first time your dog or puppy vomits up a viscous pile of bright-yellow bile, it's understandably a bit of a shocker. And any vomiting shouldn't be dismissed, as it can be a sign of a serious problem.

But oftentimes, if your dog is acting otherwise perky and normal, what you're seeing is a dog relieving himself of a build up of bile in his empty stomach. When "grazing" outside, dogs sometimes nibble grass, which also promotes bilous vomiting if the dog hasn't had his meal yet. Since the vomiting is caused by an empty stomach, you can often eliminate it with a simple diet change: Change your dog's feeding schedule, or offer two meals instead of one during the day.

Poop Patrol

It sounds gross, but making sure your dog's stools are consistent and normal is an important part of monitoring her health. For many who feed a home-prepared and/or raw diet, and like to add a carb source, quinoa is becoming an increasingly popular option. Just know, though, that the cooked germ has a curled appearance that can easily be mistaken for a parasite, such as a roundworm, in the stool – yet another reason not to panic.

Don't Risk It

Ridgebacks can be real stoics, and it can be hard to tell if they are in pain or feeling poorly. Your best bet is to pay close attention to your dog when she is healthy – note subtle things, like how she holds her body, the quality of her coat, the vibrancy in her eyes – so you can notice when she's not feeling her best.

Here are some red flags that, depending on the situation, might prompt you to seek out veterinary intervention.

Vomiting and diarrhea. Just like the rest of us, dogs can pick up viruses, or eat something that upsets their stomach. Chances are that yours will eventually experience some intestinal disturbance down the line that will clear up just as quickly as it appeared.

That said, vomiting and/or diarrhea can be symptoms of a number of serious conditions, from an infectious disease like parvovirus to an intestinal blockage. Pay close attention to how often your Ridgeback is getting sick, and what the vomit or diarrhea looks like – for instance, do you see blood? When in doubt, head to the vet.

My biggest nightmare is a Ridgeback who swallows a corn cob: Once ingested, corn cobs cannot be broken down, and unless they are surgically removed, they will cause infection and, ultimately, death. Anytime you serve corn on the cob, make sure the dogs do not have any access to the food or the garbage.

Lack of appetite. Most Ridgebacks are unrepentant chow hounds. They will countersurf, pre-lick the dishwasher contents, basically sell their souls for even a morsel of something edible. When one of them turns down food, something is wrong. Very wrong.

If one of my dogs becomes "inappetant," I watch very closely. Sometimes he truly has eaten something that doesn't agree with him, but if that's the case, within a few hours he'll usually regain his taste for food. If he doesn't within a reasonable period of time – maximum 24 hours, usually half that – it's off to the vet we go.

High fever. The only way to confirm that your dog has a fever is to take her temperature. Since thermometer chomps make an oral reading way too impractical, you'll have to do this rectally. For obvious reasons, designate a particular thermometer for this purpose. (I

Ridgebacks are stoics, and by the time they are acting ill, they could be in serious trouble. *Photo: ThruMarzenasLens.com*

write the word "DOGS" in big black-marker letters on the clear-plastic housing.)

Normal body temperature for a dog is higher than that of a human – between 101 and 102.5 F. One concern if the temperature begins to creep up beyond that is an infection of some kind. A veterinary exam, very likely followed by bloodwork, is a must.

Pale gums. We don't often think of it, but a dog's gums are an excellent barometer of his health. They should be a nice shade of pink – think bubble gum. Look at them now, when your dog is feeling fine, to get a sense of what they should look like. When you press your finger on your dog's gum, it should turn white and then back to pink as the blood refills the tissue. (I'm assuming that your Ridgeback is comfortable with this type of handling. If he's a puppy, you should insist on it; if he's an adult who is very resistant to the idea, seek out a trainer to work on getting him to accept simple handling and grooming.) Gums that look white, gray or purple are a sign that something is wrong.

Looking "off." This is probably the "squishiest" assessment of all, but arguably one of the most important. You live with your dog day in and out, and you know when he's "not acting like himself." It might be something very subtle, like a mopey attitude, or a barely visible hitch in his gait. Don't undersell your instinct: If you think something is wrong, it probably is.

Puppy Countdown

Here's a checklist for welcoming your new Ridgeback puppy:

☑ *Veterinarian.* Begin interviewing vets if you do not already have one, or touch base with your current vet to inform her of your puppy's impending arrival. Ask for a list of the vaccines that your vet gives puppies; one "shot" may contain multiple vaccines.

☑ *Nutrition.* What food will you be feeding? Ask your breeder what she feeds, and find out how you can get a supply to have some continuity for your new addition.

☑ *Puppy Kindergarten.* Enroll your puppy in a socialization class especially for youngsters. Check out a class before you commit to make sure you are comfortable with the teaching style.

☑ *Puppy playdates.* To maximize his socialization, you want your Ridgeback to meet as many appropriate dogs as possible. Make a list of neighbors and friends who have well-adjusted pooches. When you ask, "Is your dog good with other dogs?" be sure to hear the answer. Responses like "I think so," "He usually is" or "I have no idea" mean you should look elsewhere.

☑ *Crate.* For the first six months of your puppy's life, I recommend a plastic airline crate. These are useful if you are traveling as well. Since many male Ridgebacks average about 26 to 27 inches in height, you might want to get an extra large; most females are comfortable in a large. Buy the size crate that your dog will fit into as an adult. Because a puppy should only have enough room to turn around in – any roomier and the puppy will start eliminating in the crate – you can take a cardboard box and put it at the back of the crate to take up the excess room.

☑ *Toys.* Ridgeback puppies are notorious de-stuffers, so most plush animals will not last long! A must-have is a rubber Kong toy – you can stuff it with peanut butter or Cheez Whiz, freeze it, and your puppy will lick away at it for hours.

☑ *Collar.* I recommend a martingale style, which is gentler than a choke collar and the puppy can't slip out of it.

☑ *Bigger picture.* Remember that three things are required to keep your dog's immune system vibrant through his lifetime: a good, wholesome, fresh diet; a minimal vaccination schedule; and minimal exposure to pesticides, insecticides and other toxins.

Remember that four things are required to make your puppy a happy, healthy, well-adjusted Ridgeback: consistency, positive reinforcement, firm but fair leadership, and love.

A long-time staff writer, columnist and editor at the daily Long Island newspaper *Newsday*, Denise is the recipient of two coveted Front Page awards from the Newswomen's Club of New York for her 2005 story on rescued Katrina dogs and her 2006 "Animal House" blogs on the search for Vivi the missing Westminster Whippet.

Denise is the author of *The Holistic Dog Book* (Wiley, 2003), *Getting Lucky: How One Dog Found Love and a Second Chance at Angel's Gate* (Stewart, Tabori, Chang, 2005) and *Rescue Ink* (Viking, 2009). She is the founder and publisher of *Modern Molosser*, editor-at-large of *The Ridgeback Register* and *Sighthound Review*, contributing editor to *Dog News*, and a frequent contributor to *The Whole Dog Journal*. Her other Ridgeback books include *100 Memorable Rhodesian Ridgeback Moments*, published in 2013.

A member of the Rhodesian Ridgeback Club of the United States and co-chair of its 2015 national show, Denise was the club's health-and-genetics chair and historian, and is on the board of the Morris & Essex Kennel Club. She is involved with the breed on a global level as chair of the Rhodesian Ridgeback World Congress Health Committee. Denise breeds under the Revodana prefix, and lives on Long Island with her husband Fred, their 11-year-old triplets (also known as "the two-legged litter") and three Rhodesian Ridgebacks.

questions:

- what type of crate do we have?
- need to figure out someone being home to let dog out during day
- where does dog go during day if cant be left unattended?

  (can leap over high fences, sometimes ignores electric fence bc of prey instinct)

- when do they need 2nd round of vaccine?
- when can we take the dog outside?
- when do get the dog's nails clipped?
- contact info. for breeder (what groups would she recommend to connect w — via FB, etc.)
- get doggy door for laundry room so dog can have inside/outside space (they hate being cold)
- ok for dog + cat to be near each other? what about food next to each other?
- how does she recommend clipping nails?
- how does she recommend to feed?